THE LEADER'S GUIDEBOOK

LIFE PRINCIPLES FOR WORSHIP FROM THE TABERNACLE

THE LEADER'S GUIDEBOOK

LIFE PRINCIPLES FOR WORSHIP FROM THE TABERNACLE

for the Bible-study workbook by

Wayne Barber

Eddie Rasnake

Richard Shepherd

AMG *Publishers*™
Chattanooga, TN 37422

Following God

THE LEADER'S GUIDEBOOK
LIFE PRINCIPLES FOR WORSHIP FROM THE TABERNACLE

© 2001 by Eddie Rasnake and Richard L. Shepherd

Published by AMG Publishers
All Rights Reserved.

ISBN: 0-89957-314-2

Printed in the United States of America
05 04 03 02 01 00 –S– 6 5 4 3 2 1

Preface

A Leader's Guide is for leaders. What does it mean to be a leader? The apostle Paul stands as one of the most noteworthy leaders in all of human history. In 1 Corinthians 3:10, Paul states, *"According to the grace of God which was given to me, as a wise master builder I laid a foundation, and another is building upon it. But let each man be careful how he builds upon it."* Upon close examination, that verse speaks volumes about leadership. As a small group leader you are building on a foundation laid by someone before you. What is the counsel of the Holy Spirit to us through the apostle Paul? What was he saying to the Corinthians that applies to us today?

First, Paul speaks of being a wise master builder. The Greek word he uses for master builder, *architekton*, is where we get our word, "architect." But *architekton* pictures more than simply the act of designing a building. It comes from two root words: *arche,* meaning "beginning," "origin," or "the person that begins something" and *tekton,* which means "bringing forth," "begetting," or "giving birth." *Architekton* carries the idea of one who leads forth, who goes first, who is the first to bring something to light. As a small group leader, you have the opportunity to guide people in the discovery of what it means to follow God. As you discuss each of the lessons and the people and concepts you will meet in those lessons, you and your group will learn some eternal truths about what it means to follow Jesus day by day.

Paul speaks of another aspect of being a Spirit-filled leader, and it is the essential work of *"the grace of God."* All Paul did, all he taught, every spiritual truth he helped others to see, was by the grace of God. It should be the same for you. You must depend on the Lord to be the Teacher for these lessons. By His Spirit, He will guide you in understanding His Word and His ways with His children. He will open the pages of Scripture. He alone knows the heart of each group member, and He alone has the wisdom you and your group need to walk through these lessons and to make the applications to daily life.

In 1 Corinthians 3:10, the Greek word for *"building"* refers to continuous, ongoing building, and pictures placing brick upon brick, stone upon stone. We are building day by day as we spend time with the Lord in His Word and obey what He is teaching us. As you walk through each lesson week after week, another stone can be added to the life of each group member, another truth can be built into each life, and another set of truths can be added to what God is doing in you as a group. Each group will be unique. Each week will be unique. The creativity and work of the Spirit of God will ebb and flow in different ways in each heart and in the group as a whole. You as a leader have the opportunity to encourage your group to be watching for the building work of the Spirit of God. Some insights will come when each is alone with the Lord. Other insights will not be seen until you come together as a group. The Spirit of God uses both means. It is a continuous adventure of discovering more about Him, His ways, and what it means to follow Him.

With this Leader's Guide, we want to come alongside and help you lead your small group in **following God** more closely and more consistently. Be a focused, attentive leader/builder. Paul said *"let **each** man be careful how he builds."* That means each of us. No one is exempt. As a small group facilitator, you will have the opportunity to lead others and experience one of the greatest times of building lives. Let us lead as *"careful"* builders, depending on the grace and the wisdom of God.

Following His leadership,

Wayne A. Barber
Wayne A. Barber

Eddie Rasnake
Eddie Rasnake

Richard L. Shepherd
Richard L. Shepherd

Table of Contents

How to Lead a Small Group Bible Study

Causes of a Poor Study Group

The best way to become a better discussion leader is to regularly evaluate your group discussion sessions. The most effective leaders are those who consistently look for ways to improve.

But before you start preparing for your first group session, you need to know the problem areas that will most likely weaken the effectiveness of your study group. Commit now to have the best Bible study group that you can possibly have. Ask the Lord to motivate you as a group leader and to steer you away from bad habits.

How to Guarantee a Poor Discussion Group:

1. Prepare inadequately.
2. Show improper attitude toward people in the group (lack of acceptance).
3. Fail to create an atmosphere of freedom and ease.
4. Allow the discussion to wander aimlessly.
5. Dominate the discussion yourself.
6. Let a small minority dominate the discussion.
7. Leave the discussion "in the air," so to speak, without presenting any concluding statements or some type of closure.
8. Ask too many "telling" or "trying" questions. (Don't ask individuals in your group pointed or threatening questions that might bring embarrassment to them or make them feel uncomfortable.)
9. End the discussion without adequate application points.
10. Do the same thing every time.
11. Become resentful and angry when people disagree with you. After all, you did prepare. You are the leader!
12. End the discussion with an argument.
13. Never spend any time with the members of your group other than the designated discussion meeting time.

Helpful Hints

One of the best ways to learn to be an effective Bible discussion leader is to sit under a good model. If you have had the chance to be in a group with an effective facilitator, think about the things that made him or her effective. Though you can learn much and shape many convictions from those good models, you can also glean some valuable lessons on what not to do from those who didn't do such a good job. Bill Donahue has done a good job of categorizing the leader's role in facilitating dynamic discussion into four key actions. They are easy to remember as he links them to the acrostic ACTS:

*A leader ACTS to facilitate discussions by:

Acknowledging everyone who speaks during a discussion.

Clarifying what is being said and felt.

Taking it to the group as a means of generating discussion.

Summarizing what has been said.

*Taken from *Leading Life-Changing Small Groups* ©1996 by the Willow Creek Association. Used by permission of Zondervan Publishing House.

Make a point to give each group member ample opportunity to speak. Pay close attention to any nonverbal communication (i.e. facial expressions, body language, etc.) that group members may use, showing their desire to speak. The four actions in Bill Donahue's acrostic will guarantee to increase your effectiveness, which will translate into your group getting more out of the Bible study. After all, isn't that your biggest goal?

Dealing with Talkative Timothy

Throughout your experiences of leading small Bible study groups, you will learn that there will be several stereotypes who will follow you wherever you go. One of them is **"Talkative Timothy."** He will show up in virtually every small group you will ever lead. (Sometimes this stereotype group member shows up as "Talkative Tammy.") "Talkative Timothy" talks too much, dominates the discussion time, and gives less opportunity for others to share. What do you do with a group member who talks too much? Below you will find some helpful ideas on managing the "Talkative Timothy's" in your group.

The best defense is a good offense. To deal with "Talkative Timothy" before he becomes a problem, one thing you can do is establish as a ground rule that no one can talk twice until everyone who wants to talk has spoken at least once. Another important ground rule is "no interrupting." Still another solution is to go systematically around the group, directing questions to people by name. When all else fails, you can resort to a very practical approach of sitting beside "Talkative Timothy." When you make it harder for him (or her) to make eye contact with you, you will create less chances for him to talk.

After taking one or more of these combative measures, you may find that "Timothy" is still a problem. You may need to meet with him (or her) privately. Assure him that you value his input, but remind him that you want to hear the comments of others as well. One way to diplomatically approach "Timothy" is to privately ask him to help you draw the less talkative members into the discussion. Approaching "Timothy" in this fashion may turn your dilemma into an asset. Most importantly, remember to love "Talkative Timothy."

Silent Sally

Another person who inevitably shows up is **"Silent Sally."** She doesn't readily speak up. Sometimes her silence is because she doesn't yet feel comfortable enough with the group to share her thoughts. Sometimes it is simply because she fears being rejected. Often her silence is because she is too polite to interrupt and thus is headed off at the pass each time she wants to speak by more aggressive (and less sensitive) members of the group. It is not uncommon in a mixed group to find that "Silent Sally" is married to "Talkative Timothy." (Seriously!) Don't mistakenly interpret her silence as meaning that she has nothing to contribute. Often those who are slowest to speak will offer the most meaningful contributions to the group. You can help "Silent Sally" make those significant contributions. Below are some ideas.

Make sure, first of all, that you are creating an environment that makes people comfortable. In a tactful way, direct specific questions to the less talkative in the group. Be careful though, not to put them on the spot with the more difficult or controversial questions. Become their biggest fan—make sure you cheer them on when they do share. Give them a healthy dose of affirmation. Compliment them afterward for any insightful contributions they make. You may want to sit across from them in the group so that it is easier to notice any non-verbal cues they give you when they want to speak. You should also come to their defense if another group member responds to them in a negative, stifling way. As you pray for each group member, ask that the Lord would help the quiet ones in your group to feel more at ease during the discussion time. Most of all, love "Silent Sally," and accept her as she is—even when she is silent!

Tangent Tom

We have already looked at "Talkative Timothy" and "Silent Sally." Now let's look at another of those stereotypes who always show up. Let's call this person, **"Tangent Tom."** He is the kind of guy who loves to talk even when he has nothing to say. "Tangent Tom" loves to chase rabbits regardless of where they go. When he gets the floor, you never know where the discussion will lead. You need to understand that not all tangents are bad, for sometimes much can be gained from discussion that is a little "off the beaten path." But diversions must be balanced against the purpose of the group. What is fruitful for one member may be fruitless for everyone else. Below are some ideas to help you deal with "Tangent Tom."

Evaluating Tangents

Ask yourself, "How will this tangent affect my group's chances of finishing the lesson?" Another way to measure the value of a tangent is by asking, "Is this something that will benefit all or most of the group?" You also need to determine whether there is a practical, spiritual benefit to this tangent. Paul advised Timothy to refuse foolish and ignorant speculations, knowing that they produce quarrels. (See 2 Timothy 2:23.)

Addressing Tangents:

1) Keep pace of your time, and use the time factor as your ally when addressing "Tangent Tom." Tactfully respond, "That is an interesting subject, but since our lesson is on _____, we'd better get back to our lesson if we are going to finish."

2) If the tangent is beneficial to one but fruitless to the rest of the group, offer to address that subject after class.

3) If the tangent is something that will benefit the group, you may want to say, "I'd like to talk about that more. Let's come back to that topic at the end of today's discussion, if we have time."

4) Be sure you understand what "Tangent Tom" is trying to say. It may be that he has a good and valid point, but has trouble expressing it or needs help in being more direct. Be careful not to quench someone whose heart is right, even if his methods aren't perfect. (See Proverbs 18:23.)

5) One suggestion for diffusing a strife-producing tangent is to point an imaginary shotgun at a spot outside the group and act like you are firing a shot. Then say, "That rabbit is dead. Now, where were we?"

6) If it is a continual problem, you may need to address it with this person privately.

7) Most of all, be patient with "Tangent Tom." God will use him in the group in ways that will surprise you!

Know–It-All Ned

The Scriptures are full of characters who struggled with the problem of pride. Unfortunately, pride isn't a problem reserved for the history books. It shows up today just as it did in the days the Scriptures were written. Pride is sometimes the root-problem of a know-it-all group member. **"Know-It-All Ned"** may have shown up in your group by this point. He may be an intellectual giant, or only a legend in his own mind. He can be very prideful and argumentative. "Ned" often wants his point chosen as the choice point, and he may be intolerant of any opposing views—sometimes to the point of making his displeasure known in very inappropriate ways. A discussion point tainted with the stench of pride is uninviting—no matter how well spoken! No one else in the group will want anything to do with this kind of attitude. How do you manage the "Know-It-All Ned's" who show up from time to time?

Evaluation

To deal with "Know-It-All Ned," you need to understand him. Sometimes the same type of action can be rooted in very different causes. You must ask yourself, "Why does 'Ned' come across as a know-it-all?" It may be that "Ned" has a vast reservoir of knowledge but hasn't matured in how he communicates it. Or perhaps "Ned" really doesn't know it all, but he tries to come across that way to hide his insecurities and feelings of inadequacy. Quite possibly, "Ned" is prideful and arrogant, and knows little of the Lord's ways in spite of the information and facts he has accumulated. Still another possibility is that Ned is a good man with a good heart who has a blind spot in the area of pride.

Application

"Know-It-All Ned" may be the most difficult person to deal with in your group, but God will use him in ways that will surprise you. Often it is the "Ned's" of the church that teach each of us what it means to love the unlovely in Gods strength, not our own. In 1 Thessalonians 5:14, the apostle Paul states, *"And we urge you, brethren, admonish the unruly, encourage the fainthearted, help the weak, be patient with all men."* In dealing with the "Ned's" you come across, start by assuming they are weak and need help until they give you reason to believe otherwise. Don't embarrass them by confronting them in public. Go to them in private if need be. Speak the truth in love. You may need to remind them of 1 Corinthians 13, that if we have all knowledge, but have not love, we are just making noise. First Corinthians is also where we are told, *"knowledge makes arrogant, but love edifies"* (8:1). Obviously there were some "Ned's" in the church at Corinth. If you sense that "Ned" is not weak or faint-hearted, but in fact is unruly, you will need to admonish him. Make sure you do so in private, but make sure you do it all the same. Proverbs 27:56 tells us, *"Better is open rebuke than love that is concealed. Faithful are the wounds of a friend, but deceitful are the kisses of an enemy."* Remember the last statement in 1 Thessalonians 5:14, *"be patient with all men."*

Agenda Alice

The last person we would like to introduce to you who will probably show up sooner or later is one we like to call **"Agenda Alice."** All of us from time to time can be sidetracked by our own agenda. Often the very thing we are most passionate about can be the thing that distracts us from our highest passion: Christ. Agendas often are not unbiblical, but imbalanced. At their root is usually tunnel-vision mixed with a desire for control. The small group, since it allows everyone to contribute to the discussion, affords "Agenda Alice" a platform to promote what she thinks is most important. This doesn't mean that she is wrong to avoid driving at night because opossums are being killed, but she is wrong to expect everyone to have the exact same conviction and calling that she does in the gray areas of Scripture. If not managed properly, she will either sidetrack the group from its main study objective or create a hostile environment in the group if she fails to bring people to her way of thinking. "Agenda Alice" can often be recognized by introductory catch phrases such as "Yes, but . . ." and "Well, I think. . . ." She is often critical of the group process and may become vocally critical of you. Here are some ideas on dealing with this type of person:

1) **Reaffirm** the group covenant.
   At the formation of your group you should have taken time to define some ground rules for the group. Once is not enough to discuss these matters of group etiquette. Periodically remind everyone of their mutual commitment to one another.

2) **Remember** that the best defense is a good offense.
   Don't wait until it is a problem to address a mutual vision for how the group will function.

3) **Refocus** on the task at hand.
   The clearer you explain the objective of each session, the easier it is to stick to that objective and the harder you make it for people to redirect attention toward their own agenda. Enlist the whole group in bringing the discussion back to the topic at hand. Ask questions like, "What do the rest of you think about this passage?"

4) **Remind** the group, "Remember, this week's lesson is about _____."

5) **Reprove** those who are disruptive.
   Confront the person in private to see if you can reach an understanding. Suggest another arena for the issue to be addressed such as an optional meeting for those in the group who would like to discuss the issue.

Remember the words of St. Augustine: "In essentials unity, in non-essentials liberty, in all things charity."

Adding Spice and Creativity

One of the issues you will eventually have to combat in any group Bible study is the enemy of boredom. This enemy raises its ugly head from time to time, but it shouldn't. It is wrong to bore people with the Word of God! Often boredom results when leaders allow their processes to become too predictable. As small group leaders, we tend to do the same thing in the same way every single time. Yet God the Creator, who spoke everything into existence is infinitely creative! Think about it. He is the one who not only created animals in different shapes and sizes, but different colors as well. When He created food, He didn't make it all taste or feel the same. This God of creativity lives in us. We can trust Him to give us creative ideas that will keep our group times from becoming tired and mundane. Here are some ideas:

When you think of what you can change in your Bible study, think of the five senses: (sight, sound, smell, taste, and feel).

SIGHT:
One idea would be to have a theme night with decorations. Perhaps you know someone with dramatic instincts who could dress up in costume and deliver a message from the person you are studying that week. Draw some cartoons on a marker board or handout.

SOUND:
Play some background music before your group begins. Sing a hymn together that relates to the lesson. If you know of a song that really hits the main point of the lesson, play it at the beginning or end.

SMELL:

This may be the hardest sense to involve in your Bible study, but if you think of a creative way to incorporate this sense into the lesson, you can rest assured it will be memorable for your group.

TASTE:

Some lessons will have issues that can be related to taste (e.g. unleavened bread for the Passover, etc.). What about making things less formal by having snacks while you study? Have refreshments around a theme such as "Chili Night" or "Favorite Fruits."

FEEL:

Any way you can incorporate the sense of feel into a lesson will certainly make the content more invigorating. If weather permits, add variety by moving your group outside. Whatever you do, be sure that you don't allow your Bible study to become boring!

Handling an Obviously Wrong Comment

From time to time, each of us can say stupid things. Some of us, however, are better at it than others. The apostle Peter had his share of embarrassing moments. One minute, he was on the pinnacle of success, saying, *"Thou art the Christ, the Son of the Living God"* (Matthew 16:16), and the next minute, he was putting his foot in his mouth, trying to talk Jesus out of going to the cross. Proverbs 10:19 states, *"When there are many words, transgression is unavoidable. . . ."* What do you do when someone in the group says something that is obviously wrong? First of all, remember that how you deal with a situation like this not only affects the present, but the future. Here are some ideas:

1) Let the whole group tackle it and play referee/peacemaker. Say something like, "That is an interesting thought, what do the rest of you think?"

2) Empathize. ("I've thought that before too, but the Bible says. . . .")

3) Clarify to see if what they said is what they meant. ("What I think you are saying is. . . .")

4) Ask the question again, focusing on what the Bible passage actually says.

5) Give credit for the part of the answer that is right and affirm that before dealing with what is wrong.

6) If it is a non-essential, disagree agreeably. ("I respect your opinion, but I see it differently.")
   Let it go —some things aren't important enough to make a big deal about them.

7) Love and affirm the person, even if you reject the answer.

Transitioning to the Next Study

For those of you who have completed leading a **Following God** Group Bible Study, congratulations! You have successfully navigated the waters of small group discussion. You have utilized one of the most effective tools of ministry—one that was so much a priority with Jesus, He spent most of His time there with His small group of twelve. Hopefully yours has been a very positive and rewarding experience. At this stage you may be looking forward to a break. It is not too early however, to be thinking and planning for what you will do next. Hopefully you have seen God use this study and this process for growth in the lives of those who have participated with you. As God has worked in the group, members should be motivated to ask the question, "What next?" As they do, you need to be prepared to give an answer. Realize that you have built a certain amount of momentum with your present study that will make it easier to do another. You want to take advantage of that momentum. The following suggestions may be helpful as you transition your people toward further study of God's Word.

❑ Challenge your group members to share with others what they have learned, and to encourage them to participate next time.

❑ If what to study is a group choice rather than a church-wide or ministry-wide decision made by others, you will want to allow some time for input from the group members in deciding what to do next. The more they have ownership of the study, the more they will commit to it.

❑ It is important to have some kind of a break so that everyone doesn't become study weary. At our church, we always look for natural times to start and end a study. We take the summer off as well as Christmas, and we have found that having a break brings people back with renewed vigor. Even if you don't take a break from meeting, you might take a breather from homework—or even get together just for fellowship.

❑ If you are able to end this study knowing what you will study next, some of your group members may want to get a head start on the next study. Be prepared to put books in their hands early.

❑ Make sure you end your study with a vision for more. Take some time to remind your group of the importance of the Word of God. As D. L. Moody used to say, "The only way to keep a broken vessel full is to keep the faucet running."

Evaluation
Becoming a Better Discussion Leader

The questions listed below are tools to assist you in assessing your discussion group. From time to time in the Leader's Guide, you will be advised to read through this list of evaluation questions in order to help you decide what areas need improvement in your role as group leader. Each time you read through this list, something different may catch your attention, giving you tips on how to become the best group leader that you can possibly be.

Read through these questions with an open mind, asking the Lord to prick your heart with anything specific He would want you to apply.

1. Are the group discussion sessions beginning and ending on time?

2. Am I allowing the freedom of the Holy Spirit as I lead the group in the discussion?

3. Do I hold the group accountable for doing their homework?

4. Do we always begin our sessions with prayer?

5. Is the room arranged properly (seating in a circle or semicircle, proper ventilation, adequate teaching aids)?

6. Is each individual allowed equal opportunity in the discussion?

7. Do I successfully bridle the talkative ones?

8. Am I successfully encouraging the hesitant ones to participate in the discussion?

9. Do I redirect comments and questions to involve more people in the interaction, or do I always dominate the discussion?

10. Are the discussions flowing naturally, or do they take too many "side roads" (diversions)?

11. Do I show acceptance to those who convey ideas with which I do not agree?

12. Are my questions specific, brief and clear?

13. Do my questions provoke thought, or do they only require pat answers?

14. Does each group member feel free to contribute or question, or is there a threatening or unnecessarily tense atmosphere?

15. Am I allowing time for silence and thought without making everyone feel uneasy?

16. Am I allowing the group to correct any obviously wrong conclusions that are made by others, or by myself (either intentionally to capture the group's attention or unintentionally)?

17. Do I stifle thought and discussion by assigning a question to someone before the subject of that question has even been discussed? (It will often be productive to assign a question to a specific person, but if you call on one person before you throw out a question, everyone else takes a mental vacation!)

18. Do I summarize when brevity is of the essence?

19. Can I refrain from expressing an opinion or comment that someone else in the group could just as adequately express?

20. Do I occasionally vary in my methods of conducting the discussion?

21. Am I keeping the group properly motivated?

22. Am I occasionally rotating the leadership to help others develop leadership?

23. Am I leading the group to specifically apply the truths that are learned?

24. Do I follow through by asking the group how they have applied the truths that they have learned from previous lessons?

25. Am I praying for each group member?

26. Is there a growing openness and honesty among my group members?

27. Are the group study sessions enriching the lives of my group members?

28. Have I been adequately prepared?

29. How may I be better prepared for the next lesson's group discussion?

30. Do I reach the objective set for each discussion? If not, why not? What can I do to improve?

31. Am I allowing the discussion to bog down on one point at the expense of the rest of the lesson?

32. Are the members of the group individually reaching the conclusions that I want them to reach without my having to give them the conclusions?

33. Do I encourage the group members to share what they have learned?

34. Do I encourage them to share the applications they have discovered?

35. Do I whet their appetites for next week's lesson discussion?

Getting Started
The First Meeting of Your Bible Study Group

Main Objectives of the first meeting: The first meeting is devoted to establishing your group and setting the course that you will follow through the study. Your primary goals for this session should be to . . .

❏ Establish a sense of group identity by starting to get to know one another.

❏ Define some ground rules to help make the group time as effective as possible.

❏ Get the study materials into the hands of your group members.

❏ Create a sense of excitement and motivation for the study.

❏ Give assignments for next week.

BEFORE THE SESSION

You will be most comfortable in leading this introductory session if you are prepared as much as possible for what to expect. This means becoming familiar with the place you will meet, and the content you will cover, as well as understanding any time constraints you will have.

Location—Be sure that you not only know how to find the place where you will be meeting, but also have time to examine the setup and make any adjustments to the physical arrangements. You never get a second chance to make a first impression.

Curriculum—You will want to get a copy of the study in advance of the introductory session, and it will be helpful if you do the homework for Lesson One ahead of time. This will make it easier for you to be able to explain the layout of the homework. It will also give you a contagious enthusiasm for what your group will be studying in the coming week. You will want to have enough books on hand for the number of people you expect so that they can get started right away with the study. You may be able to make arrangements with your church or local Christian Bookstore to bring copies on consignment. We would encourage you not to buy books for your members. Years of small group experience have taught that people take a study far more seriously when they make an investment in it.

Time—The type of group you are leading will determine the time format for your study. If you are doing this study for a Sunday school class or church study course, the time constraints may already be prescribed for you. In any case, ideally you will want to allow forty-five minutes to an hour for discussion.

WHAT TO EXPECT

When you embark on the journey of leading a small group Bible study, you are stepping into the stream of the work of God. You are joining in the process of helping others move toward spiritual maturity. As a small group leader, you are positioned to be a real catalyst in the lives of your group members, helping them to grow in their relationships with God. But you must remember, first and foremost, that whenever you step up to leadership in the kingdom of God, you are stepping down to serve. Jesus made it clear that leadership in the kingdom is not like leadership in the world. In Matthew 20:25, Jesus said, *"You know that the rulers of the Gentiles lord it over them, and their great men exercise authority over them."* That is the world's way to lead. But in Matthew 20:26–27, He continues, *"It is not so among you, but whoever wishes to become great among you shall be your servant, and whoever wishes to be first among you shall be your slave."* Your job as a small group leader is not to teach the group everything you have learned, but rather, to help them learn for themselves and from each other. It is a servant's role.

If you truly are to minister to the members of your group, you must start with understanding where they are, and join that with a vision of where you want to take them. In this introductory session, your group members will be experiencing several different emotions. They will be wondering, "Who is in my group?" and deciding "Do I like my group?" They will have a sense of excitement and anticipation, but also a sense of awkwardness as they try to find their place in this group. You will want to make sure that from the very beginning your group is founded with a sense of caring and acceptance. This is crucial if your group members are to open up and share what they are learning.

DURING THE SESSION

⌛ OPENING: 5–10 MINUTES
GETTING TO KNOW ONE ANOTHER

Opening Prayer—Remember that if it took the inspiration of God for people to write Scripture, it will also take His illumination for us to understand it. Have one of your group members open your time together in prayer.

Introductions—Take time to allow the group members to introduce themselves. Along with having the group members share their names, one way to add some interest is to have them add some descriptive information such as where they live or work. Just for fun, you could have them name their favorite breakfast cereal, most (or least) favorite vegetable, favorite cartoon character, their favorite city or country other than their own, etc.

Icebreaker—Take five or ten minutes to get the people comfortable in talking with each other. Since in many cases your small group will just now be getting to know one another, it will be helpful if you take some time to break the ice with some fun, non-threatening discussion. Below you will find a list of ideas for good icebreaker questions to get people talking.

_____ What is the biggest risk you have ever taken?

_____ If money were no object, where would you most like to take a vacation and why?

_____ What is your favorite way to waste time?

_____ If you weren't in the career you now have, what would have been your second choice for a career?

_____ If you could have lived in any other time, in what era or century would you have chosen to live (besides the expected spiritual answer of the time of Jesus)?

_____ If you became blind right now, what would you miss seeing the most?

_____ Who is the most famous person you've known or met?

_____ What do you miss most about being a kid?

_____ What teacher had the biggest impact on you in school (good or bad)?

_____ Of the things money can buy, what would you most like to have?

_____ What is your biggest fear?

_____ If you could give one miracle to someone else, what would it be (and to whom)?

_____ Tell about your first job.

_____ Who is the best or worst boss you ever had?

_____ Who was your hero growing up and why?

⌛ DEFINING THE GROUP: 5–10 MINUTES
SETTING SOME GROUND RULES

There are several ways you can lay the tracks on which your group can run. One is simply to hand out a list of suggested commitments the members should make to the group. Another would be to hand out 3x5 cards and have the members themselves write down two or three commitments they would like to see everyone live out. You could then compile these into the five top ones to share at the following meeting. A third option is to list three (or more) commitments you are making to the group and then ask that they make three commitments back to you in return.

Here are some ideas for the types of ground rules that make for a good small group:

Leader:

_____ To always arrive prepared

_____ To keep the group on track so you make the most of the group's time

_____ To not dominate the discussion by simply teaching the lesson

_____ To pray for the group members

_____ To not belittle or embarrass anyone's answers

_____ To bring each session to closure and end on time

Member:

_____ To do my homework

_____ To arrive on time

_____ To participate in the discussion

_____ To not cut others off as they share

_____ To respect the different views of other members

_____ To not dominate the discussion

It is possible that your group may not need to formalize a group covenant, but you should not be afraid to expect a commitment from your group members. They will all benefit from defining the group up front.

⧗ INTRODUCTION TO THE STUDY: 15–20 MINUTES

As you introduce the study to the group members, your goal is to begin to create a sense of excitement about the Bible characters and applications that will be discussed. The most important question for you to answer in this session is "Why should I study _____?" You need to be prepared to guide them to finding that answer. Take time to give a brief overview of each leson.

⧗ CLOSING: 5–10 MINUTES

❑ Give homework for next week. In addition to simply reminding the group members to do their homework, if time allows, you might give them 5–10 minutes to get started on their homework for the first lesson.

❑ Key components for closing out your time are **a)** to review anything of which you feel they should be reminded, and **b)** to close in prayer. If time allows, you may want to encourage several to pray.

LIFE PRINCIPLES FOR WORSHIP FROM THE TABERNACLE

Worship from Adam to Aaron

Principles from the Fall to the Priesthood

Memory **Romans 12:1–2** Verse

"I urge you therefore, brethren, by the mercies of God, to present your bodies a living and holy sacrifice, . . . And do not be conformed to this world, but be transformed by the renewing of your mind, that you may prove what the will of God is, that which is good and acceptable and perfect."

Before the Session

❑ Study the lesson diligently for yourself. The more impact the Word makes in your own heart, the more enthusiasm you will communicate.

❑ Spread your homework out rather than trying to cram everything into one afternoon or night. You may want to use this as your daily quiet time.

❑ As you study, write down any good discussion questions you think of as they come to mind.

❑ Be transparent before the Lord and before your group. We are all learners—that's the meaning of the word "disciple."

What to Expect

Mankind was created for fellowship with God. Before sin, everything Adam did was an act of worship. The scriptural record after the fall reveals man's attempts to come back to a place of worship with God. This particular lesson is an overview to display the big picture of worship from Adam in the Garden to Aaron and the establishment of the Tabernacle. This overview lays an important foundation and sets the context for our future study of the Tabernacle. It is quite possible that many in your group will experience new insights or rich applications from their study this week. Some will realize how far they have strayed from the Word of God. Others will be affirmed in the steps of obedience they have taken. Expect the Lord to do a fresh work in you as well as in the members of the group. He waits to show Himself strong toward *"those whose heart is fully His"* (see 1 Chronicles 16:9a). Some may have questions about this study or about the Bible. You can help them see the Scriptures as God's Word written in love. They can discover that this Book is eternal wisdom and is ever able to teach, reprove, correct, and train in righteousness (2 Timothy 3:16–17).

> **THE MAIN POINT**
> The main point of this lesson is to overview worship from creation to the priesthood and to identify common principles God reveals during this time.

During the Session

⏳ **OPENING: 5–10 MINUTES**

Opening Prayer—You or one of your group members should open your time together in prayer.

Opening Illustration—Worship that is accepted by God (see 1 Peter 2:5) is a privilege unique to the Christian. It is not a right. I am permitted to offer acceptable worship only by the grace of God.

Consider briefly the significance of worship:

It is obedience to a divine command.

It is a means of nourishing the spirit.

It assists in achieving spiritual growth.

It encourages others in their spiritual development.

It shows the world where my priorities are.

It is one way of expressing my love for God.

It is an avenue God has provided by which I can praise His name.

It is the offering of spiritual sacrifices.

It is a way of showing my thanksgiving to God for all He has done for me.

It is a period of communion with God with the world shut out entirely.

It is an experience that should make the heart of every Christian glad!

As we meet together in this course and work through this Bible study on worship, we must make it our aim not just to study worship, but actually put principles of worship into practice. Otherwise, our time spent together will have been wasted.

⧖ DISCUSSION: 30–40 MINUTES

Main Objective in Day One: The objective for today's reading is to study Adam and Eve's fall and how God reestablished worship after sin. Below are some possible discussion questions for the Day One discussion. Check which questions you will use.

____ Why do you think Adam and Eve hid after they sinned?

____ How did their efforts to cover their sin and hide from God succeed?

____ What did God do to reestablish a relationship of worship with Adam and Eve?

____ Why do you think God killed animals to clothe Adam and Eve?

Main Objective in Day Two: Day Two focuses on the fact that there is a right and a wrong way to worship God. Check which discussion questions you will use for Day Two.

____ Why do you think God accepted Abel's offering but didn't accept Cain's?

____ Do you think there is any significance to the fact that Abel's offering was an animal and Cain's was not?

____ What do you think it means that Abel's offering was made in faith?

____ What did you learn from Hebrews 12:24 about the "blood of Abel"?

Main Objective in Day Three: The main focus in Day Three is the role of obedience in worship. Check any discussion questions for Day Three that you might use.

____ What reasons did you find for Noah finding favor in the eyes of God?

____ What do you see in Noah's obedience?

____ What did you observe in Noah's worship?

____ What stood out to you from Abraham's use of the word "worship"?

Main Objective in Day Four: Day Four takes a look at all the main references to worship in Genesis and Exodus and identifies the common principle of the response of a grateful heart. In addition to any discussion questions that may have come to your mind in your studying, the following suggested questions may prove beneficial to your group session:

____ What did you see in the passages in Genesis?

____ What did you see in the passages in Exodus?

____ Why do you think worship is an act of response?

____ What else stood out to you from Day Four?

Day Five—Key Points in Application: Day Five seeks to move us into application from our study of the first four days. Check which discussion questions you will use for Day Five.

____ Can you think of any examples from others who worshiped God in their own way instead of His?

____ What are some ways it has "cost" you to worship God?

____ For what do you need to be grateful?

____ You might want to close in a time of group prayer, giving thanks to the Lord for whatever He brings to mind.

⧗ CLOSING: 5–10 MINUTES

❑ **Summarize**—Restate the key points highlighted in the class.

❑ **Preview**—Take just a few moments to preview next week's lesson.

❑ **Encourage** the group to be sure to do their homework.

❑ **Pray**—Close in prayer.

TOOLS FOR GOOD DISCUSSION

Some who are reading this have led small group Bible studies many times. Here is an important word of warning: experience alone does not make you a more effective discussion leader. In fact, experience can make you **less effective**. You see, the more experience you have the more comfortable you will be at the task. Unfortunately, for some that means becoming increasingly comfortable in doing a bad job. Taking satisfaction with mediocrity translates into taking the task less seriously. It is easy to wrongly assert that just because one is experienced, that he or she can successfully "shoot from the hip" so to speak. If you really want your members to get the most out of this study, you need to be dissatisfied with simply doing an adequate job and make it your aim to do an excellent job. A key to excellence is to regularly evaluate yourself to see that you are still doing all that you want to be doing. We have prepared a list of over thirty evaluation questions for you to review from time to time. This list of questions can be found on page 11 in this Leader's Guide. The examination questions will help to jog your memory and, hopefully, will become an effective aid in improving the quality of your group discussion. Review the evaluation questions list, and jot down two or three action points below for you to begin implementing next week.

ACTION POINTS:

1. _____
_____
2. _____
_____
3. _____
_____

Where We Meet God

WALKING WHERE GOD IS TRULY WORSHIPED

MEMORY **I Corinthians 6:19–20** VERSE

"Or do you not know that your body is a temple of the Holy Spirit who is in you, whom you have from God, and that you are not your own? For you have been bought with a price: therefore glorify God in your body."

BEFORE THE SESSION

- ❑ Remember that your goal is not to teach the lesson, but to facilitate discussion.

- ❑ Additional study: You will benefit from loking at all the references to worship in Scripture, in both the Old and New Testaments. You may want to look in a concordance to see all the times the word "worship" is used. You can conduct this overview quickly, or you can take an extended time to look at these references and the context in which the accounts of worship are found.

- ❑ Make sure your own heart is a place of worship. Your surrender to the Lord will be an example and an encouragement to others in your group. Be willing to be transparent with the group about your own walk and what God is showing you about your worship and walk with Him. This will make it easier for them to open up.

- ❑ Don't be afraid of chasing tangents for a while if the diversions capture the interest of the group as a whole, but don't sacrifice the rest of the group to belabor the questions of one member. Trust God to lead you.

- ❑ You may want to keep a highlight pen handy as you study to mark key statements that stand out to you.

WHAT TO EXPECT

In this lesson there are many places at which to look, many people with which to deal; but each place and each person have some common characteristics. Each place and the heart of each person who has truly worshiped is a place of surrender to God. Wherever we see surrender, that is a place of worship. That surrender grows and deepens as we walk with the Lord. It is important for your group to understand this truth. Some may see one person's surrender as insignificant and another's as profound. Such logic is a trap of presumption. Surrender means giving all I know of myself to all I know of God—that knowledge grows as we follow God. As you look at each place of worship in this lesson, look at how God deals with each person. Look for those application points—those touch points to where each of us lives. Your small group time can become a time of worship, and the place you meet can become a place of worship.

THE MAIN POINT

Worship is about surrender from the heart, not about a particular place. It is not about a tent of animal skins or a temple of stones. God is interested in the temple of the heart.

DURING THE SESSION

⧖ OPENING: 5–10 MINUTES

Opening Prayer—Ask someone in your group to open the session in prayer.

Opening Illustration—Why Places Are Well-Known. If a person mentions Gettysburg, people think of the Civil War battle fought there or Lincoln's famous Gettysburg address. If a person mentions the Alamo, people think of the battle fought there. If a person mentions Bethel, people think of the place where God met Jacob in a dream; Bethlehem—the birthplace of Jesus; Nazareth—the boyhood home of Jesus, Armageddon—the prophesied final battleground in human history; Patmos—the island where the apostle John received the Revelation; Galatia, Ephesus, Thessalonica or Philippi—the cities or areas associated with letters from Paul. When we think of a place and what happened there it becomes noteworthy in some way. When we think of our own journey with the Lord and look back at the places we have been, what places can we remember where the Lord met us in a special way, when our faith and worship moved to a new level? What about the place where we bowed and asked Him to come into our lives as Lord and Savior? Or places along the way where He met us and dealt with us about an area of surrender that needed to take place in our lives? Any place where He pinpointed something in our lives—that place is a touch point with God, a place that we look back on as a meeting place with God. He wants every place to be a place of meeting Him, of true worship and real faith. As you walk through this lesson, think of these places in your life and about your surrender. Even the place you are in now could become a place of fresh surrender and pure worship.

⧖ DISCUSSION: 30–40 MINUTES

Once your group gets talking, you will find that all you need to do is keep the group directed and flowing with a question or two or a pointed observation. You are the gatekeeper of discussion. Don't be afraid to ask someone to elaborate further or to ask a quiet member of the group what they think of someone else's comments. Time will not allow you to discuss every single question in the lesson one at a time. Instead, make it your goal to cover the main ideas of each day, and help the group to personally share what they learned. You don't have to use all the discussion questions. They are there for your discretion.

Main Objective in Day One: In Day One, the central objective of the study is to paint a picture of what a place of worship looks like and how sacrifice and surrender enter into that picture. We want to see how the men and women of old responded to God in those places. Below, check any discussion questions that you might consider using in your group session.

____ Describe your thoughts about worship in the Garden of Eden before and after sin entered?

____ God revealed Himself to Abram. How does God use His Word in your life to reveal Himself and call you to worship?

____ How does God point out areas of fresh surrender? Can you name something that God has spoken to you about recently?

____ How does God test our faith today? How have you faced tests about your own walk? How is your group doing at walking in the fear of the Lord, or in withholding nothing from the Lord, or in obeying what He has said?

Main Objective in Day Two: In Day Two, we see how God met Moses and revealed how He wanted to dwell with His people and how they were to follow Him in true worship. Below, check which discussion questions you will use for Day Two.

____ What makes a place "holy ground"? How does God want our lives to be "holy ground"?

____ How important is the Word of God in knowing how to worship the Lord? What did God's Law do for Moses and the children of Israel?

____ Why do you think God gave so much detail in the construction of the Tabernacle? Why didn't He simply let the people build whatever they thought best?

____ What did the presence of God mean to Moses, Aaron, and the people? How would you describe what happened in Exodus 40 when the Lord appeared?

____ Are there any other areas of Day Two that you would like to discuss?

Main Objective in Day Three: Day Three takes us further into the history of Israel and opens up more of the plan of God for His people. Here we see the place of the Temple and the essential place of the life and ministry of Jesus. Look over the discussion-starter questions below to see if any are applicable to your group session.

____ What similarities do you see in the building of the Tabernacle and the building of the Temple in Jerusalem? How did God respond when the Temple was completed?

____ Thinking of the Temple as a place of prayer, what applications do you see for your walk of worship and for your prayer life?

____ Jesus revealed Himself (and God the Father and God the Spirit) so that He could be known personally. How does this match what we see in the Tabernacle and in the Temple?

____ What does the word "Immanuel" and the phrase "the Word made flesh" mean to you now?

____ Did today's lesson raise any questions for you?

Main Objective in Day Four: Day Four shows us the Temple God dwells in today—the heart and life of one who places his or her faith in Jesus Christ as Lord and Savior. Review the discussion question list below, and choose any that you feel are good questions for your session.

____ What similarities do you see between the Tabernacle, the Temple, and the life of a believer in Jesus?

____ What does it mean to you that you can be a temple of the Holy Spirit?

____ Why does God always deal with sin and forgiveness before He deals with His presence in a place or in a person's life?

____ Do you have any questions about how to deal with sin?

____ Do you have any questions about how God wants to be seen in your life?

Day Five—Key Points in Application: In looking at

"Where We Meet God," we must see what that means for everyday life. God wants His presence to be very real for each of His children—He is a Father who wants His children to walk with Him in all of life, all of the time, in every place. Some good application questions for Day Five include . . .

____ What kind of place does your heart need to be for God to want to meet there?

____ What can clutter a meeting place? What can be distracting when you are trying to meet with or talk to someone?

____ What will the fullness of the Spirit look like in a person's life? (Galatians 5:22–26 give added insight to what a person looks like when he or she is walking in the fullness of the Spirit.)

⏳ CLOSING: 5–10 MINUTES

❑ **Summarize**—Restate the key points that were highlighted in the class.

❑ **Remind** the group that the victorious Christian life is not attained when we try hard to be like Jesus, but only when we surrender our lives to God and let Him work through us.

❑ **Preview**—Take time to preview next week's lesson on **"Enter His Gates: Principles from the Fence, the Gate, and the Outer Court."** Encourage your group members to complete their homework.

❑ **Pray**—Close in prayer.

⚒ TOOLS FOR GOOD DISCUSSION ⚒

Bill Donahue, in his book, *Leading Life-Changing Small Groups* (Grand Rapids: Zondervan Publishing House, 1996), lists four facilitator actions that will produce dynamic discussion. These four actions are easy to remember because they are linked through the acrostic method to the word, **"ACTS."** You will profit from taking time to review this information in the "Helpful Hints" section of **How to Lead a Small Group Bible Study,** which is on page 5 of this Leader's Guide book.

Enter His Gates

PRINCIPLES FROM THE FENCE, THE GATE, AND THE OUTER COURT

MEMORY **Psalm 100:4** VERSE

"Enter His gates with thanksgiving and His courts with praise."

BEFORE THE SESSION

❏ Pray each day for the members of your group—that they spend time in the Word, grasp the message God wants to bring to their lives, and that they surrender to what God is saying.

❏ Do thorough preparations—don't procrastinate!

❏ As you go through the study, jot down any ideas or questions you want to discuss. Those, along with the questions listed throughout this Leader's Guide can personalize the discussion to fit your group. Think of the needs of your group, and be looking for applicable questions and discussion starters.

❏ Remain ever teachable. Look first for what God is saying to you.

❏ Be prepared to be transparent and open about what God is teaching you. Nothing is quite as contagious as the joy of discovering new treasures in the Word.

WHAT TO EXPECT

There will be varying degrees of familiarity with the Old Testament Tabernacle and its components. As we begin this week to look specifically at the parts of the structure, for some it will be review, while for others it will be entirely new. For all, it will be a new experience to look at the Tabernacle as more than a relic of ancient history. Keep drawing the focus away from the historical details and back to "What is God trying to say through the Tabernacle?" This approach will keep things practical and application-oriented.

> **THE MAIN POINT**
> In this lesson we will see what life principles can be derived from the fence, the gate, and the outer court of the Tabernacle.

DURING THE SESSION

⏳ **OPENING: 5–10 MINUTES**

Opening Prayer—Remember that the Lord is the Teacher and wants us to depend on Him as we open the Scriptures. Ask Him to teach you as you meet together.

Opening Illustration—Etched in stone over the entrance of the First Baptist Church in Warsaw, Indiana, are the words of Psalm 100:4 which state, *"Enter His gates with thanksgiving and His courts with praise."* What a good reminder to all who enter the church that we are to enter with thanksgiving and praise! But Psalm 100:4 is preceded with the final words of the previous verse, *"We are His people and the sheep of His pasture."* Question: Why would a sheep enter the gates of the Tabernacle? To give its life totally as a sacrifice. This illustration is a good reminder to all who draw near to God. This week's lesson will begin a look at what the Tabernacle teaches us about how man is to approach God.

⌛ DISCUSSION: 30–40 MINUTES

Keep the group directed along the main highway of life principles. You may have a pointed observation that helps sharpen the focus of the group. Encourage some to elaborate further on a key point or ask a quiet member of the group what they think of someone's comments. Watch the time, knowing you can't cover every single question in the lesson. Seek to cover the main ideas of each day and help the group to personally share what they have learned.

Main Objective in Day One: In Day One, the main objective is for you and your study group to see the important principle that everything in the Tabernacle is "according to pattern." Each component has a meaning and a message. Check which discussion questions you will use from Day One.

___ What is the point God is making in Exodus 25:8–9?

___ How does the epistle to Hebrews explain the meaning of the "pattern" idea in Exodus?

___ Did you learn anything else from the other verses we looked at in Hebrews?

___ What did you learn about Christ being pictured in the Old Testament?

Main Objective in Day Two: Day Two focuses on the principles being communicated about our relationship with God by the fence of the Tabernacle. The following questions may serve as excellent discussion starters for your group session:

___ Why do you think it was important to God for there to be a fence around the Tabernacle?

___ How do you think Isaiah 59:2 relates to the fence?

___ What can we gather from the verses from Revelation about the spiritual meaning of the fine white linen?

___ What else stood out to you in Day Two?

Main Objective in Day Three: Day Three introduces us to the principles being communicated about our relationship with God by the Gate of the Tabernacle. Check which discussion questions you will use from Day Three.

___ What is your initial impression of the gate of the Tabernacle?

___ What stood out to you from the New Testament Scriptures we looked at about the width of the gate?

___ It what ways is Jesus our Gate of entry to the Lord in worship?

Main Objective in Day Four: In Day Four, we look at some of the principles being communicated about our relationship with God by the bronze altar and the bronze laver. Check which discussion questions you will use from Day Four.

___ What stands out to you as you read about the bronze altar?

___ Why do you think a sacrifice is necessary to approach God?

___ What meaning do you see in the bronze laver?

___ Did you see significance in the water of the laver?

___ What else did you learn from Day Four?

Day Five—Key Points in Application: The most important component of each lesson is to move into application. Below, select a question or two for your Day Five discussion.

___ What can we do to respect God's holiness more as we approach Him?

___ Obviously we "enter the gate" initially at salvation, but what applications do you see in the gate?

___ Did you see any personal applications to the bronze altar?

___ How can we apply the bronze laver practically in our walk?

⌛ CLOSING: 5–10 MINUTES

❑ **Summarize**—Restate the key points the group shared. Review the objectives for each of the days found in these leader's notes.

- ❑ **Ask** your group to share their thoughts on the key applications from Day Five.

- ❑ **Remind**—Using the memory verse (Psalm 100:4), remind the group of the importance of how we enter God's presence.

- ❑ **Preview**—Take a few moments to preview next week's lesson, **"The Holy Place: Principles from the Lampstand, the Table, and the Altar of Incense."** Encourage your group to do their homework and to space it out over the week.

- ❑ **Pray**—Close in prayer.

TOOLS FOR GOOD DISCUSSION

One of the people who shows up in every group is a person we call **"Talkative Timothy."** Talkative Timothy tends to talk too much and dominates the discussion time by giving less opportunity for others to share. What do you do with a group member who talks too much? In the "Helpful Hints" section of **How to Lead a Small Group Bible Study** (p. 5), you'll find some practical ideas on managing the "Talkative Timothys" in your group.

4

The Holy Place

PRINCIPLES FROM THE LAMPSTAND, THE TABLE, AND THE ALTAR OF INCENSE

MEMORY **Revelation 21:3** VERSE

"The tabernacle of God is among men, and He shall dwell among them, and they shall be His people, and God Himself shall be among them."

BEFORE THE SESSION

❑ Be sure to do your own study far enough in advance so as not to be rushed. You want to allow God time to speak to you personally.

❑ Don't feel that you have to use all of the discussion questions listed for this lesson. You may have come up with others on your own, or you may find that time will not allow you to use them all. These questions are to serve you, not for you to serve.

❑ You are the gatekeeper of the discussion. Do not be afraid to "reel the group back in" if they get too far away from the lesson.

❑ Pray each day for the members of your group—that they spend time in the Word, grasp the message God wants to bring to their lives, and that they surrender to what God is saying.

WHAT TO EXPECT

Last week's lesson should have whetted the group's appetite to go further in their study of the Tabernacle. Hopefully, your group members have begun to see how practical this study can be to their daily walk with the Lord. Remember that for nearly five hun-

dred years, the Tabernacle served as a tool to instruct people on how God desires to be worshiped. Make sure you keep drawing the focus away from mere information and into application.

> ### THE MAIN POINT
> Regarding the Holy Place, we need to see what life principles can be derived from the lampstand, the table, and the altar of incense.

DURING THE SESSION

⌛ **OPENING: 5–10 MINUTES**

Opening Prayer—Remember that if it took the inspiration of God for people to write Scripture, it will also take His illumination for us to understand it. Have one of the members of your group open your time together in prayer.

Opening Illustration—In his book, *What Is Worship?* J. Vernon McGee tells of the time one of his church leaders invited him to hear a symphony orchestra perform. He said he knew nothing about music, but went anyway "to be nice."

What he first heard was a horrid cacophony of individual squeals and squawks, as each musician tuned his instrument. But then, he related, when the conductor entered the scene, what a difference there was! At his cue, all those different instruments blended their voices to create truly beautiful music.

Today, McGee explains, "every man is playing his own little tune. (But) one of these days, out from the wings will step the Conductor, the Lord Jesus Christ. And when He lifts His baton, from the ends of God's universe those galactic systems will burst forth into song. Every bird, every angel, and then man will join the heavenly chorus. In the meantime, you and I can bow before Him and bring our own little souls into the harmony of heaven."

⏳ DISCUSSION: 30–40 MINUTES

Once your group gets talking, you will find that all you need to do is keep the group directed and flowing with a question or two or a pointed observation. You are the gatekeeper of discussion. Don't be afraid to ask someone to elaborate further ("Explain what you mean, Barbara?") or to ask a quiet member of the group what they think of someone else's comments ("What do you think, Dave?"). Time will not allow you to discuss every single question in the lesson one at a time. Instead, make it your goal to cover the main ideas of each day and help the group to share what they learned personally. You don't have to use all the discussion questions below. They are there for your choosing and discretion.

Main Objective in Day One: Day One focuses on the actual structure of the tent itself and the meaning behind each piece. Below, check which discussion questions you will use from Day One.

_____ Do you think the purpose of the colors of the curtains was for symbolism or beauty or both?

_____ What do you think is God's message from the animal skins?

_____ Did anything stand out to you from the door?

Main Objective in Day Two: Day Two studies the golden lampstand and the meaning to be found in it. Check which discussion questions you will use from Day Two.

_____ What stood out to you from the looks of the lampstand?

_____ In what ways do you see Jesus pictured in the lampstand?

_____ What are some ways you see believers pictured in the lampstand and the priest's role with it?

_____ What else stood out to you from Day Two?

Main Objective in Day Three: In Day Three, we focus on the table of showbread and the meaning behind it. In addition to any discussion-starter questions that you may have in mind, the following questions may also prove useful to your group time.

_____ Did anything stand out to you from the construction of the table?

_____ What did you see suggested by a table set with food in the context of worship?

_____ What did you learn from the New Testament passages we looked at?

Main Objective in Day Four: In Day Four, we examine the altar of incense and the meaning behind it. Below, place a checkmark next to the questions that you feel are worthy of mention in your session. Or you may want to place ranking numbers next to each question to note your order of preference.

_____ What did you see in the construction of the altar of incense?

_____ What do you see in its operation?

_____ What message do you see in the burning of incense?

_____ What stood out to you from Psalm 66:18?

_____ Why do you think God dealt so harshly with Nadab and Abihu?

Day Five—Key Points in Application: Application is the most important part of each lesson. Apart from it, any study of the Tabernacle will lack in overall impact. Examine the question list below, and decide if there are any that fit your group discussion for the Day Five application time.

_____ Is there anything you need to be doing differently to make sure you are walking in the light of God's Word?

_____ What application do you see to fellowship with other Christians?

_____ How does this lesson affect how you view your prayer life?

_____ What is the main application you saw this week?

⌛ CLOSING: 5–10 MINUTES

❑ **Summarize**—Restate the key points that were highlighted in the class. You may want to briefly review the objectives for each of the days found at the beginning of these leader notes.

❑ **Focus**—Using this lesson's memory verse (Revelation 21:3), focus on the idea of the Tabernacle and God's heart toward His people.

❑ **Ask** group members to reveal their thoughts about the key applications from Day Five.

❑ **Preview**—Take a few moments to preview next week's lesson.

❑ **Pray**—Close in prayer.

TOOLS FOR GOOD DISCUSSION

As mentioned earlier, there are certain people who show up in every discussion group. Last week we looked at "Talkative Timothy." Another person who is likely to show up is **"Silent Sally."** She does not readily speak up. Sometimes, her silence is because she doesn't yet feel comfortable enough with the group to share her thoughts. Other times, it is simply because she fears being rejected. Often, her silence is because she is too polite to interrupt and thus is headed off at the pass each time she wants to speak by more aggressive (and less sensitive) members of the group. In the "Helpful Hints" section of **How to Lead a Small Group Bible Study** (p. 6), you'll find some practical ideas on managing the "Silent Sally's" in your group.

5

Enter His Presence

PRINCIPLES FROM THE VEIL, THE ARK, AND THE MERCY SEAT

MEMORY **Hebrews 10:19–22** VERSE

"Since therefore, brethren, we have confidence to enter the holy place by the blood of Jesus, by a new and living way which He inaugurated for us through the veil, that is, His flesh … let us draw near with a sincere heart in full assurance of faith…"

BEFORE THE SESSION

❑ Resist the temptation to do all your homework in one sitting or to put it off until the last minute. You will not be as prepared if you study this way.

❑ Make sure to mark down any discussion questions that come to mind as you study. Don't feel that you have to use all of the suggested discussion questions included in this leader's guide. Feel free to pick and choose based on your group and the time frame with which you are working.

❑ Remember your need to trust God with your study. The Holy Spirit is always the best teacher, so stay sensitive to Him!

WHAT TO EXPECT

In this lesson, expect that all your group members will need a better understanding of the most holy place in the Tabernacle. Anticipate that a few of your group members may not be familiar with the Old Testament at all, and *Yom Kippur* will be a new and exciting idea. Some will be surprised to discover how practical and application-filled this lesson will be. Make every effort to steer the study away from being just another lesson by reminding your group members to look to their own lives and circumstances for how these principles can apply to them.

> **THE MAIN POINT**
> The objective of studying "The Holy of Holies" is to see what life principles can be derived from the Veil, the Ark, and the Mercy Seat

DURING THE SESSION

⧗ **OPENING: 5–10 MINUTES**

Opening Prayer—Remember to have one of your group members open your time together in prayer.

Opening Illustration—A man was carried in a dream to a church. In his vision he saw the organist vigorously playing the organ, but no sound was heard. The choir and congregation began to sing, but their voices were not heard. Then the minister began, energetically, to pray, but no tones came from his lips.

The man turned in wonder to his angel guide. "You hear nothing," said the angel, "because there is nothing to hear. These people are not engaged in worship, but only in the form of worship. Their hearts are not touched, and this silence is the silence that is yet unbroken in the presence of God. But listen now."

And, listening, the man heard a child's voice, clear and distinct in all that silence, while the minister seemed to pray, and the people seemed to join. Only the child's voice was heard, because only the child's heart was touched. "That," said the guide, "is the only true worship in all this great church today: all the others are concerned with only the appearance of worship."

⏳ DISCUSSION: 30–40 MINUTES

Remember that your job is not to teach this lesson, but to facilitate discussion. Do your best to guide the group to the right answers, but don't be guilty of making a point someone else in the group could just as easily make.

Main Objective in Day One: The objective here is to gain a feel for life principles to be seen in the veil. Choose some discussion questions from the list below.

_____ What do you think the veil must have looked like to those who saw it for the first time?

_____ Do you think we should read meaning into the colors of the veil?

_____ Why do you think God wanted Cherubim on the veil?

_____ What stood out to you from Hebrews 10?

Main Objective in Day Two: In Day Two, we begin looking at the meaning in the ark of the covenant. Below, check any discussion questions you might use from Day Two.

_____ What stands out to you most about the ark?

_____ Why do you think God dealt so harshly with the man who touched the ark?

_____ What do you think the Philistines were trying to do when they stole the ark?

_____ Did today's study raise any questions for you?

Main Objective in Day Three: Day Three takes a look at the items that were placed inside the ark and their significance. Review the questions below, and see if any are suitable to your group discussion on Day Three.

_____ Why did God want the "testimony" placed in the ark?

_____ What stands out to you from the manna being placed inside?

_____ What message do you think God is sending by putting Aaron's rod in the ark?

_____ Did anything else grab your attention in your studies in Day Three?

Main Objective in Day Four: In Day Four, we see the key component of the mercy seat and its message to us. Check which discussion questions you will use from Day Four.

_____ What did you find out in 1 John 2?

_____ Did you see a message in the Cherubim over the mercy seat?

_____ What else stood out to you from Day Four?

Day Five—Key Points in Application: The important thing to see out of Day Five is that we need to apply these principles to our own lives. Decide on some discussion-starter topics for the application section of Day Five. The following questions are suggested questions that you may want to use for your discussion:

_____ Has your view of the Tabernacle changed through looking at the components?

_____ How has your view of sin changed through this study?

_____ Were there any areas in particular where this lesson touched your heart?

⏳ CLOSING: 5–10 MINUTES

❑ **Summarize**—Go over the key points of your study of the Holy of Holies.

❑ **Remind** group members that living a victorious Christian life is not attained when we try hard to be like Jesus, but only when we surrender our lives to God and let Him work through us.

❑ **Ask** them what they thought were the key applications from Day Five.

❑ **Preview**—Take a few moments to preview next week's lesson. Encourage group members to complete their homework.

❑ **Pray**—Close in prayer.

TOOLS FOR GOOD DISCUSSION

Hopefully your group is functioning smoothly at this point, but perhaps you recognize the need for improvement. In either case, you will benefit from taking the time to evaluate yourself and your group. Without evaluation, you will judge your group on subjective emotions. You may think everything is fine and miss some opportunities to improve your effectiveness. You may be discouraged by problems you are confronting when you ought to be encouraged that you are doing the right things and making progress. A healthy Bible-study group is not one without problems, but is one that recognizes its problems and deals with them the right way. At this point in the course, as you and your group are nearly halfway-completed with the study of the Tabernacle as it relates to worship, it is important to examine yourself and see if there are any mid-course corrections that you feel are necessary to implement.

Review the evaluation questions list found on page 11 of this Leader's Guide, and jot down two or three action points for you to begin implementing next week. Perhaps you have made steady improvements since the first time you answered the evaluation questions at the beginning of the course. If so, your improvements should challenge you to be an even better group leader for the final seven lessons in the study.

ACTION POINTS:

1. _____

_____

2. _____

_____

3. _____

_____

6

Ministers to the Lord

PRINCIPLES FROM THE PRIESTHOOD

MEMORY **I Peter 2:9** VERSE

"But you are a chosen race, a royal priesthood, a holy nation, a people for God's own posses-sion, that you may proclaim the excellencies of Him who has called you out of darkness into His marvelous light"

BEFORE THE SESSION

❑ Remember the Boy Scout motto: **BE PRE-PARED!** The main reason a Bible study floun-ders is because the leader comes in unprepared and tries to "shoot from the hip."

❑ Walk through the discussion questions below, looking at your lesson and selecting which questions you will use.

❑ Make sure to jot down any discussion questions that come to mind as you study.

❑ Don't forget to pray for the members of your group and for your time studying together. You don't want to be satisfied with what you can do—you want to see God do what only He can do!

WHAT TO EXPECT

In studying this lesson, you should realize that all of us are called to be priests to our God and to serve Him in some way. Be prepared for your group to need to overcome a mentality of applying this only to clergy and missionaries. As we look at the priest-hood we should see ourselves. Be sensitive to any discussion questions that may surface in this lesson, and guard your group from applying the principles only to others rather than to themselves.

THE MAIN POINT
There are life principles to be learned for our own walk with God from studying the Old Testament priests.

DURING THE SESSION

⧖ **OPENING: 5–10 MINUTES**

Opening Prayer—Remember to have one of your group members open your time together in prayer.

Opening Illustration—Bill Smith. There may be no name more common in the English language. In a seminary class, one professor related an event that happened his first day in college.

His teacher professed an uncanny command of the English language. It seemed that he always pulled out the most appropriate word for the occasion. On this, the first day of school, he was calling the roll. After recognizing each student he made some perti-nent comment about his name—its history, mean-ing, or some historically-related story. Finally, he came to Bill Smith. He said with a pause and in a reflective tone, "Bill Smith . . . that is a common name." Stirred from within, Bill arose from his seat and said in a loving but firm tone, "Sir, Bill Smith may be frequent but not common."

Who among us has not lived under the teacher's philosophy? Thinking there is nothing special about ourselves, we have concluded that we are common, everyday, ordinary. Let us continually remind ourselves that each one of us is a chosen person, a royal priest, a member of a holy nation, a person that belongs to God (1 Peter 2:9).

⏳ DISCUSSION: 30–40 MINUTES

Remember to pace your discussion so that you will be able to bring closure to the lesson at the designated time. You are the one who must balance lively discussion with timely redirection to ensure that you don't end up finishing only part of the lesson.

Main Objective in Day One: In Day One, the main objective is to see that God is behind the appointment of the priests. No one is self-appointed. Check which discussion questions you will use from Day One.

_____ What do you think it means that Aaron and his sons were to minister as priests to the Lord?

_____ How did God involve others in His affirmation of Aaron?

_____ What stood out to you from the passage in Hebrews about the role of priests?

_____ What else stood out to you from your study in Day One?

Main Objective in Day Two: In Day Two, we learn some of the significance of the priestly apparel. Choose a discussion question or two from the Day Two list below.

_____ What stood out to you from your reading in Exodus 28?

_____ Why do you think God was so concerned with how the priests looked?

_____ Did anything particular grab you from the various parts of the priest's apparel?

_____ Did your study of Day Two raise any questions for you?

Main Objective in Day Three: Day Three introduces us to a brief overview of the priestly activity. This will be discussed in more detail later. Decide on some discussion-starter questions for your session on priestly activity. Below, are some possible discussion questions for you to consider.

_____ Why do you think God instituted sacrifices to become a part of man's worship?

_____ What stood out to you from Hebrews 5:2 about the priestly oversight?

_____ What did you learn from Nehemiah 8:1–3?

Main Objective in Day Four: In Day Four, we see the most significant activity of the priest—*Yom Kippur,* the Day of Atonement. This will be looked at again before we finish, but there are many practical applications here for us. Check which discussion questions you will use from Day Four.

_____ What did God desire the attitude of the people to be on Yom Kippur?

_____ What message do you see in the fact that it was observed year after year?

_____ How do you think the principle of Yom Kippur applies to us today?

_____ Did you learn anything new in comparing the Old and New covenants?

Day Five—Key Points in Application: Although there are many different applications to the priesthood, some of these will be pursued in another lesson. This time we chose to camp on the idea of seeking God's will, which was a priestly activity using the *Urim* and *Thummim.* Below, check any discussion questions that are best suited to your group for application.

_____ The priests often sought God's will for themselves and the people. Have you ever thought of God's will as a privilege to all through the priesthood of believers?

_____ What do you think about the formula, "Desire + Opportunity + No Red Flags"?

_____ What other applications did you see in this week's lesson?

⏳ CLOSING: 5–10 MINUTES

❑ **Summarize**—Restate the key points.

❑ **Remind** those in your group that living a victorious Christian life is not attained when we try hard to be like Jesus, but only when we surrender our lives to God and let Him work through us.

❑ **Preview**—Take a few moments to preview next week's lesson. Encourage your group to do their homework and to space it out over the week.

❑ **Pray**—Close in prayer.

 ## TOOLS FOR GOOD DISCUSSION

As discussed earlier, there are certain people who show up in every discussion group that you will ever lead. We have already looked at "Talkative Timothy" and "Silent Sally." This week, let's talk about another person who also tends to show up.

Let's call this person **"Tangent Tom."** He is the kind of guy who loves to talk even when he has nothing to say. Tangent Tom loves to "chase rabbits" regardless of where they go. When he gets the floor, you never know where the discussion will lead. You need to understand that not all tangents are bad. Sometimes, much can be gained from discussion "a little off the beaten path." But these diversions must be balanced against the purpose of the group. In the "Helpful Hints" section of **How to Lead a Small Group** (p. 6), you will find some practical ideas on managing the "Tangent Toms" in your group. You will also get some helpful information on evaluating tangents as they arise.

The Debt of Sin

DEALING WITH SIN GOD'S WAY

MEMORY **I Peter 2:24** VERSE

"And He Himself bore our sins in His body on the cross, that we might die to sin and live to righteousness;..."

BEFORE THE SESSION

❑ Try to get your lesson plans and homework done early this week. This gives time for you to reflect on what you have learned and process it mentally. Don't succumb to the temptation to procrastinate.

❑ Make sure you keep a highlight pen handy to highlight any things you intend to discuss; including questions that you think your group may have trouble comprehending. Jot down any good discussion questions that come to your mind as you study.

❑ Don't think of your ministry to the members of your group as something that only takes place during your group time. Pray for your group members by name during the week that they would receive spiritual enrichment from doing their daily homework. Encourage them as you have opportunity.

WHAT TO EXPECT

In this lesson we look at two essential offerings, the sin offering and the guilt offering. These may be foreign ideas or seem like ancient (even unimportant) rituals to some in your group. The important thing to remem-

ber in walking through your discussion time is the heart of the matter—we must deal with sin if we are to know God and walk with Him. There are many pictures and principles God reveals through these offerings. Expect that everyone in your group will have areas of their life to which these principles will apply in some way. Be prepared to share your own journey as well as guide them toward personal evaluation of their lives and personal application to the different areas of their lives. Remember, when dealing with sin, the circle of confession is as big as the circle of offense. You and the members of your group can be an encouragement to one another to walk in the forgiveness and cleansing God wants for each of us.

> **THE MAIN POINT**
> God requires us to deal with sin, and He has made full provision for us to do so—not just to admit sin, but to find His full forgiveness.

DURING THE SESSION

⌛ **OPENING: 5–10 MINUTES**

Opening Prayer—It would be a good idea to have a different group member each week open your time together in prayer.

Opening Illustration—Many have heard of the hymn "It is Well with My Soul" and the tragedy that birthed it. Horatio Spafford, a lawyer and teacher, scheduled a trip to France for his family and himself, but he had to delay going because of business. He sent his wife and four daughters on to France aboard the *Ville du Havre,* planning to join them soon after. The ship collided with another vessel in the mid-Atlantic and sunk within an hour. The four daughters drowned, and their mother sent a cablegram, with the brief message, "saved alone." The four daughters had been converted in a meeting led by Dwight L. Moody in Chicago, and Mr. and Mrs. Spafford experienced great peace and strength, knowing that their daughters were in heaven. Horatio Spafford penned the words to "It Is Well with My Soul" after that tragedy. Many quote the words to the first verse, "When peace, like a river, attendeth my way, When sorrows like sea-billows roll; Whatever my lot, Thou hast taught me to say, 'It is well, it is well with my soul.' " The third verse speaks to a peace that goes beyond the temporal tragedy they faced. It is the peace of sin forgiven. Think of these words, "My sin—oh, the bliss of this glorious thought, My sin—not in part, but the whole, Is nailed to the cross and I bear it no more, Praise the Lord, praise the Lord, O my soul!" Horatio Spafford's burden of sin and guilt was an even greater burden to him than the children he had lost at sea. Yet, Mr. Spafford and his wife could know the peace of God for the grief of his soul over his children and for the burden of sin that had been taken care of by the Lord. His heart was calmed by the work of Christ on the Cross. Horatio knew the peace that only God could bring. That is the message of the sin offering and the guilt offering. These offerings were established so that the peace of forgiveness could be established between God and His people.

⌛ DISCUSSION: 30–40 MINUTES

A key objective in how you manage your discussion time is to keep the big picture in view. Your job is not like a schoolteacher's job, grading papers and tests and the like, but more like a tutor's job, making sure your group understands the subject. Keep the main point of the lesson in view, and make sure they take that main point home with them.

Main Objective in Day One: In Day One, the main objective is to see the importance of dealing with sin

God's way so that man can walk with God in the right way. Start thinking now about what discussion starters you will use in your session devoted to dealing with sin. Review the question list below. Perhaps there is a question or two below that might be essential to your group time.

_____ What insights do you see in the fact that God initiated the various offerings and how they were to be offered?

_____ Why do your think it was important to have these offerings given on a regular basis?

_____ What new insights did you see in the procedures associated with the sin offering?

_____ How important is it to God that we deal with sin? How important should it be to each one of us?

_____ What else stood out to you from Day One?

Main Objective in Day Two: In Day Two, we see the importance of making any offense right with God first, then making right any offense against another person. Check which discussion questions you will use from Day Two.

_____ How big does an offense have to be to be an offense? What insights did you see in the ten offenses given in Leviticus 5 and 6?

_____ How important is restitution to God? Do you want things made right or restitution given when you have been offended, wronged, or robbed in some way?

_____ How did you respond the last time that you faced an offense? What about the last time you offended someone? [You may want to use this as a thought-provoking question, since some would not want to tell of an offense within the group meeting.]

_____ Why is it important to deal with offenses quickly? How valuable is a "conscience void of offense"?

Be sensitive to the Spirit of God in walking through this lesson. There may be someone in your group that is wrestling with this issue of dealing with sin, especially dealing with restitution. Ask the Lord to lead you as you talk through these truths.

Main Objective in Day Three: Day Three looks at the importance of the sin offerings on the Day of

Atonement. Of even greater importance is how the Lord Jesus Christ fulfilled the will of God as our sin offering, thus taking away our sins. Take a look at the discussion question list below to see if any are applicable to your group session.

_____ What does it mean to treat the Lord as holy? How can we do that or fail to do that today?

_____ The Lord had to sensitize His people to the seriousness of sin and the importance of walking clean before Him. The Day of Atonement was one of the most important times for picturing clean living to the people. What in that Day shows you the seriousness of sin and dealing with it?

_____ What does God use today to show us the seriousness of sin? How can we help one another deal with sin more consistently?

_____ What insights about the Lord Jesus as our sin offering were especially meaningful to you?

_____ Were there any questions raised by your study in Day Three?

Main Objective in Day Four: Day Four examines Isaiah 52 and 53 and looks at how the Lord Jesus fulfills the guilt offering pictured there. He is our substitute for sin, a truth we must hold dearly and a reality in which we must walk. Choose some discussion starters for your group session.

_____ What do you see in Isaiah that reminds you of the things Jesus faced during His time on earth?

_____ What insights about judgment on sin do you see in Isaiah 53?

_____ What insights about the love of the Servant for you and me do you see in Isaiah 53?

_____ What do you think it was like as Philip and the Ethiopian traveled and discussed the Scriptures about this Suffering Servant? Discuss some of the things Phillip may have told him.

Day Five—Key Points in Application: The most important application point out of Day Five is the opportunity to experience not only the forgiveness of the Lord, but also His joyful presence. After all,

He made us for His enjoyment. Below, check any discussion questions that you might consider using for your application time.

_____ What, for you, is the most inviting aspect of the presence of the Lord?

_____ What is the most damaging aspect of sin as far as your daily life goes?

_____ What keeps us from dealing with sin quickly and thoroughly? What can we do to encourage one another to deal fully with any and every sin, any and every time it comes up?

_____ What is the strongest application point you observed this week?

⌛ CLOSING: 5–10 MINUTES

❑ **Summarize**—You may want to read "The Main Point" statement at the beginning of the leader's notes on "The Debt of Sin.

❑ **Preview**—If time allows, preview next week's lesson on "The Devotion of Surrender: Walking in the Joy of Surrender to Jesus Christ." Encourage your group to complete their homework.

❑ **Pray**—Close in prayer.

TOOLS FOR GOOD DISCUSSION

One of the issues you will eventually have to combat in any group Bible study is the enemy of **boredom.** This enemy raises its ugly head from time to time, but it shouldn't. It is wrong to bore people with the Word of God! Often boredom results when leaders allow their processes to become too predictable. As small group leaders, we tend to do the same thing in the same way every single time. Yet God the Creator, who spoke everything into existence, is infinitely creative! Think about it. He is the one who not only created animals in different shapes and sizes, but different colors as well. When He created food, He didn't make it all taste or feel the same. This God of creativity lives in us. We can trust Him to give us creative ideas that will keep our group times from becoming tired and mundane. In the "Helpful Hints" section of **How to Lead a Small Group** (pp. 8–9), you'll find some practical ideas on adding spice and creativity to your study time.

The Devotion of Surrender

WALKING IN THE JOY OF SURRENDER TO JESUS CHRIST

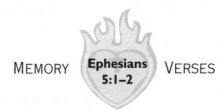

MEMORY **Ephesians 5:1–2** VERSES

"Therefore be imitators of God, as beloved children; and walk in love, just as Christ also loved you, and gave Himself up for us, an offering and a sacrifice to God as a fragrant aroma."

BEFORE THE SESSION

❑ Your own preparation is key not only to your effectiveness in leading the group session, but also in your confidence in leading. It is hard to be confident if you know you are unprepared. These discussion questions and leader's notes are meant to be a helpful addition to your own study but should never become a substitute.

❑ As an aid in your study of the offerings or for further study, you may benefit from looking over the chart "General Overview of the Offerings in the Tabernacle and the Temple" at the end of Lesson 7 in the workbook (p. 105).

❑ As you do your homework, study with a view to your own relationship with God. Resist the temptation to bypass this self-evaluation on your way to preparing to lead the group. Nothing will minister to your group more than the testimony of your own walk with God.

❑ Don't think of your ministry to the members of your group as something that only takes place during your group time. Pray for your group members by name during the week that they would receive spiritual enrichment from doing their daily homework. Encourage them as you have opportunity.

WHAT TO EXPECT

As with the sin offering and the guilt offering of Lesson 7, the offerings covered in this lesson may be foreign to many of the members of your group. The burnt, grain, drink, and peace offerings may seem like ancient (even unimportant) rituals, but as in the sin or guilt offerings the important thing to remember is the heart of the matter—God delights in hearts surrendered to Him and His will. He delights to work through surrendered lives. These offerings give us vivid pictures and life-changing principles for our walk with God and what it means to follow Him with a whole heart. Expect that each person in your group will have areas of their life to which these principles apply in some way. Be prepared to share your own journey as well as guide them toward personal evaluation. Remember, God is continually moving us to new depths of surrender and to a greater capacity to know Him in His fullness. Your time in "The Devotion of Surrender" can be an opportunity for each one to better evaluate where he or she is. This can also be a time of encouragement to grow in surrender. Be open to challenge the members of your group to become that daily "burnt offering"—a living sacrifice, yielded, broken, and poured out.

During the Session

⧗ OPENING: 5–10 MINUTES

Opening Prayer—A good prayer with which to open your time is the prayer of David in Psalm 119:18, *"Open my eyes, that I may behold wonderful things from Thy law."* Remember that if it took the inspiration of God for men to write Scripture, it will take His illumination for us to understand it.

Opening Illustration—When one country surrenders to another after a war there is often what is called an "unconditional surrender." There is a deep peace in existence as long the unconditional surrender lasts. The same thing is true in our surrender to the Lord. In the Tabernacle, twice each day the burnt offering was offered up, a twice–daily reminder of surrender. Every day we must see the importance of surrender—a moment-by-moment, hour-by-hour, day-by-day, yielding up of our hearts and lives to the Lord to follow Him whatever our circumstance. The word "circumstance" pictures the "circle" (circum) in which you "stand." Regardless of the condition of the day or the circumstances we face, there can be a heart attitude and a life action of surrender. That can be followed by the experience of peace with God as well as the peace of God, from God. We can walk in that peace, know that peace, and enjoy that peace.

As you walk through the burnt offering and the grain and drink offerings that accompanied it, the devotion of surrender as well as the picture of the peace of surrender will become clearer. That is what God wants for us each day, all day.

⧗ DISCUSSION: 30–40 MINUTES

Remember to pace your discussion so that you don't run out of time to get to the application questions in Day Five. This time for application is perhaps the most important part of your Bible study. It will be helpful if you are familiar enough with the lesson to be able to prioritize the days for which you want

to place more emphasis, so that you are prepared to reflect this added emphasis in the time you devote to that particular day's reading.

Main Objective in Day One: In Day One, the main objective is to understand the significance of the burnt offering and how it pictures daily surrender to the Lord as well as to His ways and His will. Choose a discussion question or two from the Day One list below.

_____ What aspects of the burnt offering grabbed your attention?

_____ What does the fact of a twice-daily burnt offering say to you about your daily walk with the Lord?

_____ Anyone could offer a burnt offering, poor or rich. The poor were unable to offer a rich person's offering, but were instructed to offer what they could. The rich were to offer what they could afford as well. What does this say to you about how God views surrender?

_____ Are there any other thoughts from Day One that you would like to discuss?

Main Objective in Day Two: We learn in Day Two the meaning of the grain and drink offerings and how they picture surrender to the Lord. Check which discussion questions you will use from Day Two.

_____ What stands out to you about the grain or the drink offerings?

_____ What are some of the elements of "yeast" or "honey" that can get mixed in with our walk of surrender?

_____ How important is it to keep our focus on the Lord in offering ourselves to Him, especially when that involves our service for others—as a drink offering? What could get in the way of our service?

Main Objective in Day Three: Day Three introduces us to the "peace offering" showing us the peace we can walk in as a result of dealing with sin and walking in surrender to the Lord. In addition to any discussion questions you may have in mind for your group session, the following questions below may also be useful:

_____ What stands out to you about the peace or fellowship offering?

_____ What does the peace offering say to you about how the Lord wants to fellowship with us and wants us to fellowship with Him?

_____ Proverbs 17:1 says, *"Better is a dry morsel and quietness with it than a house full of feasting with strife."* What common elements to the experience of the peace offering do you see?

_____ What difference does Jesus make in how we experience the peace of God or peace with one another?

_____ Were there any other questions raised by your study in Day Three?

Main Objective in Day Four: In Day Four, we see how the Lord Jesus perfectly fulfilled all the "sweet aroma" offerings—the burnt offering, the grain offering, the drink offering, and the peace offering. Place a checkmark next to the discussion question you would like to use for your group session. Or you may want to place a ranking number in each blank to note your order of preference.

_____ What stands out to you about Jesus as our "sweet aroma" offering?

_____ What was the most important thing about the offerings according to Jesus?

_____ How can we get caught up in the outward forms of religion and miss the heart of what God is saying or wanting?

_____ What does it mean to you that Jesus offered all of Himself for you? What do you see in His actions that showed surrender to the Father's will and love for us?

_____ Are there other insights gained or questions raised from Day Four?

Day Five—Key Points in Application: The most important application point from Day Five is how Jesus' offering of Himself paved the way for us to truly worship God and walk with Him in joyous fellowship. Make sure your members understand all Jesus has done and how it applies to each of us. Check which discussion questions you will use from Day Five.

_____ How does seeing the mercies of God (Romans 1–11) help us walk as a living sacrifice (Romans 12:1–2)?

_____ How does Jesus' daily walk of surrender to His Father encourage you in your walk of surrender?

_____ What are some of the ways we can present offerings to the Lord today?

_____ What other applications did you see from this week?

⧖ CLOSING: 5–10 MINUTES

❑ **Summarize**—Restate the key points. You may want to reread "The Main Point" statement for "The Devotion of Surrender."

❑ **Preview**—Take time to preview next week's lesson on **"Positioning for Worship: God's Order for Transporting and Positioning of the Tabernacle."** Encourage your group members to do their homework.

❑ **Pray**—Close in prayer.

✂ TOOLS FOR GOOD DISCUSSION ⚒

From time to time, each of us can say stupid things. Some of us, however, are better at it than others. The apostle Peter certainly had his share of embarrassing moments. One minute, he was on the pinnacle of success, saying, *"Thou art the Christ, the Son of the Living God"* (Matthew 16:16), and the next minute, he was putting his foot in his mouth, trying to talk Jesus out of going to the cross. Proverbs 10:19 states, *"When there are many words, transgression is unavoidable. . . ."* What do you do when someone in the group says something that is obviously wrong? First of all, remember that how you deal with a situation like this not only affects the present, but also the future. In the "Helpful Hints" section of **How to Lead a Small Group** (p. 9), you'll find some practical ideas on managing the obviously wrong comments that show up in your group.

9

Positioning for Worship

GOD'S ORDER FOR TRANSPORTING AND POSITIONING THE TABERNACLE

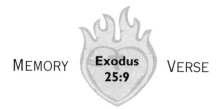

MEMORY **Exodus 25:9** VERSE

"According to all that I am going to show you, as the pattern of the tabernacle and the pattern of all its furniture, just so you shall construct it."

BEFORE THE SESSION

❏ Pray each day for the members of your group—that they spend time in the Word, grasp the message God wants to bring to their lives, and that they surrender to what God is saying.

❏ Be sure you have searched the Scriptures carefully for each day's lesson.

❏ While preparing for this lesson, read through the discussion questions on the following pages and select which questions you will use.

❏ Remain ever teachable. Look first for what God is saying to you. This will help you in understanding and relating to some of the struggles that your group members may be facing as they are seeking to make an impact on those around them.

WHAT TO EXPECT

Studying the issue of the positioning of the Tabernacle can at first appear to be one of the less interesting lessons in this study, but when you realize that there is meaning and purpose in every detail, finding that meaning and purpose will be a joy. Expect the members of your group to be surprised at how many prac-

tical applications there are to be found in this component of the Tabernacle. Make sure to be sensitive to those group members who did not find those applications on their own. Make sure everyone leaves with a sense of what God is saying.

> **THE MAIN POINT**
> Since God is so specific on different issues of positioning, we will find that He has a purpose and a message for us.

DURING THE SESSION

⧗ **OPENING: 5–10 MINUTES**

Opening Prayer—Remember to ask the Lord for **His** wisdom. He promised to guide us into the truth.

Opening Illustration—Dr. Philip Brooks often told the story of a missionary who, while home on furlough, wanted to find something to take back to his mission post—something that would be accepted by all the natives. He finally decided upon securing a rather large bronze sundial. When he returned, he called the natives together, and they helped him set the dial in proper position. Then the missionary explained its function. The natives were all very pleased and very much interested. A few days later, the missionary was astonished to find that the natives had built a shelter over the sundial to protect it. Their lack of understanding rendered the sundial useless. You see, it is the positioning of the sundial that enables it to tell us what it is designed to tell us. In the same way, the positioning of the Tabernacle was essential for it to communicate what God intended.

⌛ DISCUSSION: 30–40 MINUTES

Select one or two specific questions to get the group started. By this point in the course (Week Nine), you know the talkative ones and the ones who are quiet. Continue to encourage each member in the importance of his or her input. Some of the greatest applications ever to be learned from this study course may come from someone who has said very little up to this point.

Main Objective in Day One: In Day One, the main objective is to set forward the significance of the Tabernacle as the centerpiece of the camp. Review the question list below, and decide upon some discussion starters for your group session.

_____ Why do you think God was so specific about the placement of the Tabernacle?

_____ What message do you see in it being always in the center of the camp?

_____ What did you think about the "cross" idea in the placement of the tents?

_____ What does this lesson speak to you about your own worship of God?

Main Objective in Day Two: Day Two focuses on the significance of the Tabernacle always being positioned facing East and what God is saying through that. Check which discussion questions you will use from Day Two.

_____ Did anything in particular stand out to you from Exodus 26:18–22?

_____ What did you see in Isaiah 64:8?

_____ What pattern did you see from the Scriptures we reviewed for Day Two?

_____ Why is it important that the path toward the Tabernacle was always due west?

_____ Did anything else stand out to you from today's homework?

Main Objective in Day Three: Day Three is a review of the High Priest's path as he made his progression from the gate of the Tabernacle to the Holy of Holies. Each item that the High Priest passed contains a message concerning our approach to God. Some good discussion questions for Day Three include . . .

_____ What stands out to you from the High Priest's path and the items found in the outer court of the Tabernacle?

_____ What meaning do you see in the three items in the Holy Place?

_____ What is the point of the Holy of Holies being the innermost room?

_____ Did anything else grab you from today's study?

Main Objective in Day Four: Day Four examines the final component of the Tabernacle's positioning—how it was carried—and looks for applications to our worship. Check which discussion questions you will use from Day Four.

_____ Why do you think God had the Israelites follow a pillar?

_____ Why do you think Judah was first in line behind the pillar?

_____ What significance do you see in the placement of the ark?

_____ Did today's lesson raise any pertinent questions for you?

Day Five—Key Points in Application: The most important application point in this lesson is to begin looking at the path of the priest as a model for our approach to God. Below, are some suggestions for discussion questions. Feel free to come up with your own questions as well.

_____ As you consider the challenges of walking with God today, which of the areas listed in your books make it difficult for you personally to keep the Lord at the center of your life?

_____ Do you see any changes you need to make as a result of this lesson?

_____ As you looked at the steps in the process of the priest moving toward God, which did you find most meaningful?

⏳ CLOSING: 5–10 MINUTES

- **Summarize**—Restate the key points the group shared. Review the objectives for each of the days found in the leader's notes for Lesson Nine.

- **Focus**—Make sure the group sees the importance of each reference in regards to positioning of the Tabernacle.

- **Ask** them to express their thoughts about the key applications from Day Five.

- **Encourage**—We have finished nine lessons. This is no time to slack off. Encourage your group to keep up the pace. We have three more lessons full of life-changing truths. Take a few moments to preview next week's lesson. Encourage your group members to do their homework in proper fashion by spacing it out over the week.

- **Pray**—Close in prayer.

TOOLS FOR GOOD DISCUSSION

The Scriptures are replete with examples of people who struggled with the problem of pride. Unfortunately, pride isn't a problem reserved for the history books. It shows up just as often today as it did in the days the Scriptures were written. In your group discussions, you may see traces of pride manifested in a "know-it-all" group member. **"Know-It-All Ned"** may have shown up in your group by this point. He may be an intellectual giant, or he may be a legend only in his own mind. He can be very prideful and argumentative. If you want some helpful hints on how to deal with "Know-It-All Ned," look in the "Helpful Hints" section of **How to Lead a Small Group Bible Study** (p. 7).

10

False Worship

DISOBEDIENCE TO GOD'S ORDER FOR WORSHIP AND ITS CONSEQUENCES

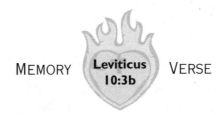

MEMORY **Leviticus 10:3b** VERSE

"By those who come near to Me I will be treated as holy, and before all the people I will be honored."

BEFORE THE SESSION

❑ Never underestimate the importance of prayer for yourself and for the members of your group. Ask the Lord to give your group members understanding in their time in the Word and to bring them to a new level of knowing Him.

❑ Spread your study time over the week.

❑ Remember to mark those ideas and questions you want to discuss or ask as you go through the study.

❑ Be sensitive to the needs of your group. Be prepared to stop and pray for a member who may be facing a difficult struggle or challenge.

WHAT TO EXPECT

Expect that your group not only needs to understand truths in this area of false worship, but also needs to be challenged to evaluate their own worship in that light. Hopefully by this time, the pieces are beginning to fit together and they have begun looking at everything as it applies to them. Encourage them not to miss this important step of application. Next week, we will look at positive examples of worship, but there is much to be gained from a study of negative examples as well.

THE MAIN POINT
There is a wrong way to worship, and there are consequences to not following God's revealed will.

DURING THE SESSION

⏳ **OPENING: 5–10 MINUTES**

Opening Prayer—Have one of the group members open the time with prayer.

Opening Illustration—On April 25, 1994, the news section of *Christianity Today,* reported that some fans of Elvis Presley were actually revering the king of rock and roll as a god. Pockets of semi-organized Elvis worship had taken hold in New York, Colorado, and Indiana. Worshipers raised their hands, spelled and then chanted Presley's name, worked themselves into a fervor, and prayed to the deceased star. Followers believe Elvis watches over them. If someone reports seeing Presley, the high priests at the Church of the Risen Elvis in Denver hold Elvis worship services. They enshrined a look-alike doll of Elvis in an altar surrounded by candles and flowers. This illustration is proof positive that just because something is called worship does not mean it is acceptable to God. Many times man worships the wrong thing or in the wrong way.

⏳ DISCUSSION: 30–40 MINUTES

Select one or two specific questions to get the group started in discussion. Continue to encourage each member in the importance of his or her insights and input.

Main Objective in Day One: Day One looks at the incident of false worship during the early days of the Tabernacle—worship of the golden calf—and looks for applications to us. Good discussion starters for Day One include . . .

_____ What were the leaders supposed to do while Moses was on the mountain, meeting with God?

_____ What did they do and what resulted?

_____ Do you see dangers that relate to our worship?

_____ What stood out to you from the sin and how God dealt with it?

Main Objective in Day Two: In Day Two, the main objective is to see God's dealings with Nadab and Abihu in light of the point God is making about worship. Below are some suggested questions for your discussion on Day Two. Which questions will you use for your group session?

_____ What was the sin of Nadab and Abihu, and how did God deal with it?

_____ Why do you think God dealt with their sin so severely?

_____ What stood out to you from the story of Ananias and Saphira?

_____ What do these examples say of our worship?

Main Objective in Day Three: In Day Three, the objective is to identify principles of worship from Korah's rebellion. What discussion starters do you plan to use for Day Three? Here are some suggestions:

_____ What was Korah's complaint?

_____ What is wrong with his perspective?

_____ What does this incident of Korah teach us about potential hindrances to our worship?

_____ What else stood out to you from Day Three?

Main Objective in Day Four: Day Four looks at the mistakes in worship by King Saul at Gilgal and how they apply to us. Check which questions you will use for your discussion on Day Four.

_____ What stands out to you from Saul's actions here?

_____ Why do you think God doesn't credit him for at least being partially obedient?

_____ What do you see in Saul's responses to Samuel that reflect a lack of true repentance?

_____ What else stood out to you from Day Four?

Day Five—Key Points in Application: The most important aspect of each lesson is taking time to seek to apply the truths to our own lives. Make sure you save time for this important part. Select a discussion question or two from the list below.

_____ What are some examples you have seen of worship that was not according to truth?

_____ What idols stood out to you from the list that are a temptation today?

_____ What are some ways you have seen the Lord not honored or treated in holy in worship?

_____ What are some ways we are tempted to grumble against leaders?

⏳ CLOSING: 5–10 MINUTES

❑ **Summarize**—Review the key points the group shared. You may want to review "The Main Point" statement for this lesson. Also, ask your group to express their thoughts about the key applications from Day Five.

❑ **Focus**—Using the memory verse (Leviticus 10:3), focus the group on the heart of true worship and the importance of guarding against false worship.

❑ **Preview**—Take a few moments to preview next week's lesson on True Worship.

❑ **Pray**—Close in prayer.

 ## TOOLS FOR GOOD DISCUSSION

So, group leaders, how have the first nine weeks of this study been for you? Have you dealt with anyone in your group called **"Agenda Alice?"** She is the type that is focused on a Christian "hot-button" issue instead of the Bible study. If not managed properly, she (or he) will either sidetrack the group from its main study objective, or create a hostile environment in the group if she fails to bring people to her way of thinking. For help with "Agenda Alice," see the "Helpful Hints" section of **How to Lead a Small Group Bible Study** (pp. 7–8).

11

True Worship

WORSHIPING GOD IN SPIRIT AND IN TRUTH

MEMORY **Philippians 3:3** VERSE

"For we are the true circumcision, who worship in the Spirit of God and glory in Christ Jesus and put no confidence in the flesh."

BEFORE THE SESSION

❑ Pray for your group as they study through this week's lesson.

❑ Spread your study time over the week. This is like a large meal. You need time to chew each truth and digest it fully.

❑ As you walk through this lesson on true worship, continually keep in mind the contrast with false worship, even as the golden calf incident stands in sharp contrast to the events surrounding Moses and the Tabernacle in Exodus 25—40. This will help in guiding the discussion on true worship with your group.

❑ As you study, remember to jot down those ideas and questions you want to discuss or ask as you go through this lesson with your small group.

WHAT TO EXPECT

Knowing facts and figures about the Tabernacle or the Temple is useless if we do not apply these truths to our hearts, especially to our personal worship of the true God. God still seeks those who will worship Him in spirit and truth. This lesson looks at the big picture all the way from Genesis to Revelation. It will be important to help your group see the big pic-

ture without getting lost in the details. At the same time, it is essential to help focus the group on personal application of all we have seen in these eleven lessons.

Help your group see the importance of finishing what God has called them to do—even finishing this study in *Following God*. (We have only one more lesson to go after this lesson.) Encourage them to share insights that God has shown them.

> ### THE MAIN POINT
> We are to worship God in spirit and in truth, never depending on the flesh or straying into deceptive traps of idolatry and false worship.

DURING THE SESSION

⧗ OPENING: 5–10 MINUTES

Opening Prayer—Have one of the group members open the time with prayer.

Opening Illustration—Acts 17:16–34 give us one of the clearest illustrations of the importance of true worship in all of Scripture. There we see Paul declaring the matter of true worship versus false worship as a matter of life and death, even eternal life versus eternal death. He knew it was a matter for which there is ultimate accountability to Jesus Christ, the resurrected Lord. When Paul talked to the Athenians, he spoke of their altar to the "Unknown God," an altar that appeared to be "god-insurance"— they wanted to make sure there was no god that they were potentially offending by not having an altar devoted to him. In their thinking, an unrecognized god could bring a plague or famine or catastrophe, so they covered their bases by devoting an altar to any gods they failed to acknowledge. The idea of worship to them was a sobering, fearful matter; yet they understood nothing about the true God and true worship. They knew worship was important in life, but they did not have the full picture. Paul brought that full picture to them showing them they must walk in true worship. That meant walking with God, honoring Jesus Christ as resurrected Lord and Savior. The people responded in three different ways: some sneered; some wanted to hear more later; and some joined themselves to Paul and to the Lord, or literally, they glued themselves to Paul in belief and trust of this true God. Telling others about true worship versus false worship will have the same results in our day. It is a matter of life or death . . . forever. You and your group can know the reality of true worship as you follow the Lord God of heaven and His Son Jesus. You can lead others to do the same.

⏳ DISCUSSION: 30–40 MINUTES

Study diligently in your preparation time. This will help you guide the discussion as well as answer many of the questions that arise in your group. Knowing the ways of God in guiding us in true worship can help your group in many areas of their Christian walk. True worship is the foundation upon which everything else rests. It is where we start and never leave. As you trek through the lesson, seek to keep the main point the main point and be sure to leave time for the application points in Day Five. There is nothing more important than emphasizing personal application in worship.

Main Objective in Day One: In Day One, the main objective is to see that in seeking those who will worship Him in spirit and truth the Father focuses on the true condition of each heart. In addition to any discussion questions you may have in mind, the list of questions below may also contain useful discussion-starter ideas.

_____ How do we try to hide sin, either in what we have done or what is in our hearts? Why do we think we can hide from God?

_____ What effect can truth have on one's heart and life? How can being truthful or honest with God affect our attitude, our countenance, or our ability to make wise choices?

_____ How important is wisdom in our walk with God or in our worship of Him?

_____ How does our worship affect others? How does true worship (with true wisdom) affect our relationships with others?

Main Objective in Day Two: In Day Two, the main objective is to see how the Lord Jesus began to guide the woman of Samaria into the truth and to true worship. Check which discussion questions you will use from Day Two.

_____ How does knowing Jesus as the Giver affect how we ask things of Him?

_____ Jesus began with the woman at the well by focusing on a need (water) and how He could more than meet that need. Why would He focus on this need first?

_____ Why did Jesus bring up the woman's sin? How does He do that with us? How does personal sin relate to the issue of true worship?

_____ How do we try to change the subject with the Lord? Can you think of ways we substitute religion for true worship? How can we guard against substitutes for true worship?

Main Objective in Day Three: In Day Three, our main objective is to see how Jesus reveals Himself so that we can worship Him in spirit and truth. Below, are some suggested discussion starters for you to consider.

_____ True worship magnifies who the Lord is in our eyes. How was Jesus magnified in the woman's eyes?

_____ How do we see sin when we see the Lord for Who He is?

_____ What effect does seeing the Lord for Who He is have on our lives? What effect does seeing the Lord for Who He is have in relationships with others?

_____ Think of how the Lord desires truth in relationships—first with Him and then with others. How important is truth to you in the relationships you have (at home, at school, at work, in business dealings, at church)?

Main Objective in Day Four: Day Four's main objective is for you and your group to see how the Holy Spirit leads true worshipers in a walk of true worship. Check any questions that are applicable for your Day Four-discussion time.

_____ What does the picture of the Spirit being like living water say to you? How does this encourage you?

_____ What does it take to receive living water?

_____ How is the Spirit like refreshing water?

_____ What options are left open to those who refuse Jesus' offer of living water? What kind of life can they expect to live? What kind of eternity will they have?

Day Five—Key Points in Application: The most important application point in "True Worship" is found in fulfilling the purpose for which God created us—to know Him and the fullness of His Life. When we know this we can experience the joy of His presence and point others to Him so they too can know Him and His fullness of Life. Check which discussion questions you will use to help focus the applications from Day Five.

_____ How are true worship and the fullness of the Holy Spirit connected?

_____ What part does the Holy Spirit play in guiding us in true worship? What are some ways He leads us in worship?

_____ What are some of the things that keep us from true worship or from being controlled by the Holy Spirit?

_____ True worship can be "a little heaven on earth." Describe what that could look like.

⧗ CLOSING: 5–10 MINUTES

❑ **Summarize**—Restate the key points the group shared.

❑ **Focus**—Using the memory verse (Philippians 3:3), focus the group again on what it means to worship God in truth. Remind the members of your group that life is meant to be lived by His Spirit's fullness, by His power, wisdom, and grace.

❑ **Ask** them to share their thoughts about the key applications from Day Five.

❑ **Preview**—Take a few moments to preview next week's lesson on **"Jesus Christ, Our High Priest: Leading Us into True Worship and Fellowship with God."** Encourage your group members to do their homework in proper fashion by spacing it out over the week.

❑ **Pray**—Close in prayer.

⚒ TOOLS FOR GOOD DISCUSSION ⚒

Well, it is evaluation time again! You may be saying to yourself, "Why bother evaluating at the end? If I did a bad job, it is too late to do anything about it now!" Well, it may be too late to change how you did on this course, but it is never too late to learn from this course what will help you on the next. Howard Hendricks, that peerless communicator from Dallas Theological Seminary, puts it this way: "The good teacher's greatest threat is satisfaction—the failure to keep asking, 'How can I improve?' The greatest threat to your ministry is **your ministry.**" Any self-examination should be an accounting of your own strengths and weaknesses. As you consider your strengths and weaknesses, take some time to read through the evaluation questions list found in **How to Lead a Small Group Bible Study** on pages 11–12 of this leader's guide. Make it your aim to continue growing as a discussion leader. Jot down below two or three action points for you to implement in future classes.

ACTION POINTS:

1. _____

_____

2. _____

_____

3. _____

_____

12

Christ, Our High Priest

LEADING US INTO TRUE WORSHIP AND FELLOWSHIP WITH GOD

MEMORY **Hebrews 10:19–22** VERSES

"Since . . . we have confidence to enter the holy place by the blood of Jesus, by a new and living way which He inaugurated for us through the veil, that is, His flesh, and since we have a great priest over the house of God, let us draw near. . . , having our hearts sprinkled clean from an evil conscience and our bodies washed with pure water."

BEFORE THE SESSION

❏ You will certainly need to pray for your group as they walk through this final lesson in the study, *Life Principles for Worship from the Tabernacle*. Ask the Lord to give clear insight into who Christ is as our High Priest. Never underestimate the importance of prayer for yourself and for the members of your group. Pray for each of them by name.

❏ Spread your study time over the week.

❏ Remember to mark those ideas and questions you want to discuss or ask as you go through the study. Add to those some of the suggested questions listed on the following pages.

❏ To better see the Person of Christ you may want to look at the lessons that refer to Christ in other Following God studies: "Adam: Following God's Design" (Lesson 1) in *Following God: Life Principles from the Old Testament,* "Christ the Prophet: Worshiping in Spirit and Truth" (Lesson 12) in *Following God: Life Principles from the Prophets of the Old Testament,* "The True King in Israel: Following the King of Kings" (Lesson 12) in *Following God: Life Principles from the Kings of the Old Testament,* "The Bride of Christ: Walking in the Beauty of

Holiness" (Lesson 12) in *Following God: Life Principles from the Women of the Bible Book One,* and "The Son of Man: Following His Father" (Lesson 12) in *Following God: Life Principles from the New Testament Men of Faith.*

❏ Be sensitive to the working of the Spirit in your group meeting, ever watching for ways to help one another truly follow and worship God.

WHAT TO EXPECT

We know that Jesus is Savior and Lord, but many times we forget about or fail to see the significance and importance of Jesus' role as High Priest. Many in your group will have little or no understanding of the priesthood, especially the place and role of the High Priest. Many will think of some modern form of priesthood or a priesthood from history which is foreign to the Old and New Testament ideas. When coupled with an understanding of the Tabernacle, the priesthood, and the offerings, the place of the High Priest can have great personal meaning for the members of your group. You may need to review some of the truths learned in Lessons 1–11 on the Tabernacle, priesthood, and offerings. This will help you to better explain or clarify these truths or answer questions that arise during your discussion time.

The Scriptures have much to say about Jesus as our High Priest and perfect sacrifice. Many in your group will gain new insights into Christ's work of salvation and how it applies to each of them. Hopefully, they will see many new application points for walking with Him as **their** High Priest. Encourage them to share their insights as you guide the discussion.

> ### THE MAIN POINT
> Jesus Christ, through the fullness of both His Person and His work, brings us to Himself in salvation and to true worship and fellowship.

DURING THE SESSION

⧗ OPENING: 5–10 MINUTES

Opening Prayer—Psalm 119:18 says, *"Open my eyes, that I may behold wonderful things from Thy law."* Ask the Lord to open your eyes as you meet together. Have one of the group members open the time with prayer.

Opening Illustration—Following to the Finish. I was driving on an Interstate highway one morning and got stuck in traffic. It was a time for enduring not enjoying. In the midst of that the Lord showed me a very important truth. Right in front of me was a car with the words "I Love Running" surrounding the car tag. Obviously an avid jogger owned this. On the left side of the back bumper was a half-sized bumper sticker with these words in bold print: "I FINISHED—RiverRun 15 K." This person had run the required fifteen kilometers of the RiverRun 15K and finished—no word about who won the race, or how long it took to complete their run, just that this person **finished**. What a powerful truth! That is what the book of Hebrews urges its readers. You and I are running a race. Sometimes we want to quit, to back out, but the Lord is saying keep running, keep trusting, keep looking to Jesus, the author and finisher of faith (Hebrews 12:2). For the joy set before Him, He endured the cross and has sat down at the right hand of the throne of God. You endure. It will be worth all the effort, all the struggle, all you have to face, because the rewards are far greater than

any received for finishing a 15K run, for they are eternal! During your Christian "run," you can know the joy of fellowship with God and experience true worship.

As your group has looked at **Jesus Christ, Our High Priest**, each one has seen how He is our sovereign Lord, one who sympathizes with each of us, one who sacrificed Himself for us, and one who is ever strong and able to give us His strength to run the race. This lesson can be a strong encouragement to look to the Lord for strength, to focus on Him, and in so doing, to follow Him in fellowship all the way to the finish. He calls us to come into the Holy of Holies and live in His presence. Help the members of your group determine to follow to the finish.

⧗ DISCUSSION: 30–40 MINUTES

Select one or two specific questions to get the group started. This lesson on Christ, our High Priest offers many application points about how each of us is following and worshiping the Lord. He is continually guiding us in worshiping Him, and we need to encourage one another in true worship. Remember to look for those "Velcro" points where members can see something that applies to their own lives. Encourage them to share the insights the Lord has shown them during the week.

Main Objective in Day One: In Day One, the main objective is to see our High Priest as the sovereign Lord who is worthy of worship and to whom we must pay close attention. Place a checkmark next to the suggested discussion questions that you would like to use in your group session. Or you may want to use ranking numbers and rank the questions in preferential order.

_____ What are some of the characteristics of the Son of God? Which ones are most meaningful to you?

_____ What do you think it would be like to follow one who ruled with a righteous scepter, who followed God's will in every detail?

_____ What are some ways we can pay close attention to the Lord and what He has spoken?

_____ What are some things that can get in the way of listening to God and His Word? How can we neglect hearing Him and drift in our walk?

Main Objective in Day Two: In Day Two, the main objective is to see how our High Priest sympathizes with us in our sorrows, temptations, and struggles. Check which discussion questions you will use from Day Two.

_____ What stands out to you about the Lord Jesus, particularly His walk on earth, facing the many sufferings He faced?

_____ What does it mean to you that Jesus is "merciful and faithful"?

_____ What does it mean to you that Jesus faced the full force of every kind of temptation? What does that mean when you face temptation?

_____ How does the invitation to come to the throne of grace motivate you in following Jesus?

Main Objective in Day Three: Day Three focuses on our sacrificial High Priest and the work He accomplished through the cross. Some good discussion questions for Day Three include these.

_____ Someone has compared the sacrifices of the Old Testament to a credit card—using the credit card covers the payment for a time, but does not pay for the item or service. The debt still has to be paid when the bill comes. What does it mean to you that Jesus paid your sin debt—no bill will ever come?

_____ What difference should it make in your daily walk knowing that God wants you to come into His presence with confidence or boldness through the blood of Jesus? How should this affect your prayer time? Your decision-making process?

_____ What does it mean to you that you have been set apart in a special class by the sacrifice of Jesus?

_____ What other insights have you gleaned from Day Three?

Main Objective in Day Four: In Day Four, the main objective is to see our strong High Priest and how He wants to be our strength for daily life. Select a discussion question or two from the list of questions below.

_____ The key element in faith is **the object of our faith** not the amount of faith. As someone has pointed out, "thin faith" in "thick ice" is more important than "thick faith" in "thin ice" if you want to walk across an ice-covered lake. What insights have you gleaned about how Abraham grew and how we grow strong in faith?

_____ Even in the face of His trials, Jesus knew He was both Lord and High Priest, and that His Kingdom and His sacrificial work would stand. What insights and/or personal applications do you see about Jesus' strength in the events surrounding His trials, crucifixion, and resurrection, especially as they apply to your need for strength day by day?

_____ How is the Christian life like a race? What insights have you gleaned about how to run your race?

_____ What does it really mean to be satisfied? Where is true satisfaction found according to the Scriptures?

Day Five—Key Points in Application: The most important application point seen in "Jesus Christ Our High Priest" is how His work of salvation is being carried out in each of His children. He wants us to walk with a strong faith in Him, confident in His ability to fulfill the work He has begun in us. In light of that, we can look to Him as our strength for the race set before us, and we can experience the joy of true worship and fellowship. Check which discussion questions you will use to help focus the applications from Day Five.

_____ What is God able to do? What fresh insights has God shown you about His ability, especially as it relates to you and your circumstances?

_____ What are some ways we "interact" with the Lord? Why is it vitally important to know His Word as we interact with Him in the various circumstances of life?

_____ We can get discouraged in running the race—weary, thirsty, ready to give up. How can we encourage one another in the race each of us is running?

_____ What is the most significant insight the Lord has shown you concerning Jesus as High Priest (for the present and/or for the future)?

⌛ CLOSING: 5–10 MINUTES

❑ **Summarize**—Restate the key points the group shared. Review the main objectives for each of the days found in these leader notes.

❑ **Focus**—Using the memory verses (Hebrews 10:19–22), direct the group's focus to the open door into full fellowship and worship we have through the Lord Jesus, our High Priest. Note the practical applications to everyday life that His High Priesthood has for each one.

❑ **Ask** the group to express their thoughts about the key applications from Day Five.

❑ **Pray**—Close your time in prayer, thanking the Lord for the journey He has led you on over the past twelve weeks.

 TOOLS FOR GOOD DISCUSSION

Congratulations! You have successfully navigated the waters of small group discussion. You have finished all twelve lessons in *Following God: Life Principles for Worship from the Tabernacle*, but there is so much more to learn, so many more paths to take on our journey with the Lord, so much more to discover about what it means to follow Him. Now what? It would be wise for you and your group to not stop with this study. In the front portion of this leader's guide (in the "Helpful Hints" section of **How to Lead a Small Group Bible Study,** pp. 9–10), there is information on how you can transition to the next study and share those insights with your group. Encourage your group to continue in some sort of consistent Bible study. Time in the Word is much like time at the dinner table. If we are to stay healthy, we will never get far from physical food, and if we are to stay nourished on "sound" or "healthy" doctrine, then we must stay close to the Lord's "dinner table" found in His Word. Job said it well, *"I have not departed from the command of His lips; I have treasured the words of His mouth more than my necessary food"* (Job 23:12).